FIRE ON ICE

THE EXCLUSIVE INSIDE STORY OF TONYA HARDING

ABBY HAIGHT and J.E. VADER

and the Staff of

The Oregonian

TIMES T BOOKS

RANDOM HOUSE

ISBN 0-8129-2457-6
Manufactured in the United States of America
9 8 7 6 5 4 3 2
First Edition

"If you really have a dream, you should follow it. That's what I'm doing. But I want people to remember that I'm a normal person like they are, except that I've always had a dream and I made that dream."

–TONYA HARDING, *December 1991*

Contents

Prologue

It should have been a triumphant return for Tonya Harding. On Monday evening, January 10, 1994, Harding's reign as the queen of U.S. figure skating was only forty-eight hours old. The dynamic twenty-three-year-old blonde from rural Clackamas County in Oregon had finally proven her doubters wrong and won the 1994 U.S. Figure Skating Championship, the highest accolade in the sport besides Olympic gold. Harding's victory two days before at the Joe Louis Arena in Detroit was special because it met another huge goal, a berth on the U.S. Olympic team that would compete in a month in Lillehammer, Norway.

Since she first laced up skates as a three-year-old, Tonya Harding had wanted to skate in the Olympic Games. When she was young, she had a child's dream of beauty and glory. As she aged, the dream took on a harder edge of the reality around her. An Olympic medal meant the kind of money that would wipe out a lifetime of want. When Harding looked at the Olympic rings, she saw dollar signs, she told reporters.

Harding didn't get to celebrate much in Detroit. Everyone was more concerned about the bizarre attack January 6 on Harding's rival, Nancy Kerrigan, which had forced her to drop out of the competition. The favorite to win her second title, Kerrigan was the reigning American skating queen. In the post-competition press conference, reporters wanted Harding to talk about what it felt like to win without Kerrigan. Harding wanted to talk only about her skating. Even with the gold medal around her neck, it was obvious that Harding was still in Kerrigan's shadow.

As they walked up the ramp at Portland International Airport, Harding and Jeff Gillooly, her on-again, off-again husband, were worried about the more than four hours they had spent over the last two days talking to investigators in Detroit, including an agent with the Federal Bureau of Investigation. The agent had wanted to know about the attack on Kerrigan. He had talked of trivial things for a while, then abruptly asked Gillooly if he knew someone named Derrick. Gillooly was startled. He said he didn't.

A big homecoming celebration had been planned for Harding when she arrived at Portland. Members of the Tonya Harding Fan Club had made sure the local media knew Harding's flight and time of arrival, and the information was broadcast on television newscasts and published in *The Oregonian*. More than forty members of the Portland Rosarians, a civic group, were at the airport with a proclamation from the City of Portland. Dozens of fans waited with balloons, flowers and posters that read, "Go for the gold, Tonya!"

Their wait was long and disappointing. At the last minute, Harding had changed her flight plans.

Now it was almost 9 p.m., and a couple dozen loyal fans were back at the airport. So were local reporters.

Harding and Gillooly entered the gate lobby, and a large man in a trench coat immediately stepped up behind Harding and placed a protective hand on the small of her back. The man was Shawn Eric Eckardt, a longtime friend of Gillooly's who had been hired as Harding's bodyguard. Eckardt's three-hundred-pound frame dwarfed the five-foot-one Harding as he guided her through well-wishers.

As he usually did when he and his wife were in public, Gillooly stepped back into the crowd. Television newscasts later showed the short, mustachioed Gillooly walking grimly a few feet away from Harding. Gillooly didn't stick out in a crowd, but on this night, his frowning, worried face set him apart from the happy fans.

Eckardt shepherded Harding through a small gantlet of well-wishers and reporters. Harding's training partner, seventeen-year-old Angela Meduna, had brought her friend a stuffed animal. Several people wore the lemon-yellow "Team Tonya" T-shirts that Harding herself had designed before the national championships.

The skater laughed only once, when a television cameraman, jogging backward to keep Harding in focus, crashed into a post and almost fell down.

Harding had agreed to a short press conference, and her most zealous fan, a Vietnam veteran named Joe Haran, had arranged for a small airport meeting room where the press could set up their tripods and lights. Harding, looking small in her black coat and black turtleneck shirt, her hair pulled back in a tight ponytail, sat down in front of the bright lights and cameras and waited impatiently for the first question. Ordinarily, her return to Portland after a competition would go mostly unnoticed by the Portland media. But the Kerrigan attack made that impossible. The television stations sent out their top reporters, and radio stations that had never previously mentioned Harding had their microphones ready.

Harding was tired. She had never liked talking to reporters. She was sure they would want to go over the same things she'd been talking about for days—the fear she said she felt about Kerrigan's attack, how the championship wasn't complete without her rival, how she thought she had skated great. Then a reporter asked if the FBI had asked her if she had been part of the attack on Kerrigan.

"I'm really disappointed that you guys would even ask me that," she said. "You guys know me better than that. I had my hopes for a long time of competing against Nancy and proving I'm as good as her and better." In fact, Harding said, she was looking forward to skating against Kerrigan at the Olympic Games so she could "kick her butt."

After a few minutes, Gillooly and Harding signaled that the questions were over. Harding's father, Al, had been told to wait at the main entrance of the airport, then drive his daughter to Gillooly's mother's house. Eckardt had rehearsed the plan with Al Harding several times, and when the bodyguard whisked Tonya out the doors, Al was waiting. But instead of driving off immediately with her, Al waited. "Go! Go! Go!" Eckardt screamed, until Al revved the car and sped away.

Eckardt and Gillooly followed in the bodyguard's car. It was the first time they could speak privately. Gillooly told his friend about the FBI questioning. As the pair drove toward their rendezvous with Harding at Gillooly's mother's house, they realized the plan they had created was falling apart. They would have to cover it up.

FIRE ON ICE

1

True Grit

She chose her sport at age three, taking group lessons at Silverskate, a suburban ice skating rink long since closed. Skating and the fearless little girl were a perfect fit. Within a month, Tonya Harding was able to bunny hop, glide, and skate backward—skills other kids took a year to master. Within twelve months, Harding had won her first competition, at Sun Valley, Idaho.

The story that Harding and her mother always tell is that when she was three she saw skaters at the Lloyd Center shopping mall rink. Little Tonya was entranced and begged her mother to allow her to skate. She refused to take no for an answer, she wanted to skate so much. Her mother finally relented, and after she explained that Tonya wasn't just supposed to sit on the ice and eat the shavings, off she went. And once she was moving, the future champ just didn't want to stop.

But David Kellogg, Harding's cousin, has a different story. He said that LaVona Harding was driven to turn her daughter into a skater from the start. From before the start.

"I remember her mom telling her she was going be a skater even before she was born. She said if this was a girl, she was to be a skater."

Tonya was a skater, and she was good. She also had a strong incentive to get good very quickly.

"It's impossible to forget Tonya," recalled Antje Spethmann, who took lessons with Harding. "Even then everyone saw her promise. She was great, a natural. The only problem was that horrible mother of hers."

Spethmann said LaVona Harding "was abusive and negative. She talked like a trucker and called Tonya things like 'scum,' 'bitch' and 'stupid.' This was to a little girl."

When Harding made a mistake on ice, her mother beat her, Spethmann said. "She didn't care that other kids and their mothers were there and saw what she was doing. She'd yell at Tonya, say she was making all these sacrifices and spending all this money so she could learn to skate and Tonya better be grateful. She wouldn't let Tonya come off the ice when she had to go to the bathroom. And all the time she'd be yelling that Tonya sucked. I'm telling you, she was a mother from hell."

The mother, now LaVona Golden, denied the accusations. She said she wasn't against giving a child a swat now and again, but she didn't beat and didn't spank. Her problems were just normal mother-rebellious daughter problems.

It was not an easy life. LaVona sewed costumes and waited tables at night to pay for her daughter's skating. Money was scarce; homes were just temporary things. Al Harding, Tonya's father, was unemployed for long stretches, and the blue-collar family bounced to eight different addresses. One thing remained constant for skating's most unlikely family: Mother and daughter at war.

And yet Tonya never cried or asked to quit. The kid was tough. The kid was an athlete.

"Most girls needed to be talked into doing some of the hard things," said Spethmann. "Not Tonya. She'd try anything. She was fearless. Some of the older kids in class would dare her to attempt a double lutz, and she'd try it. The falls never bothered her."

When the scandal surrounding the Nancy

5

Kerrigan attack broke, there was a hunger to know more about Harding's life, her upbringing. LaVona Golden was much discussed, much interviewed. She showed up at the Clackamas Town Center rink to watch her daughter practice in the mornings and to talk to reporters. She wore drop earrings for an interview with Connie Chung on CBS's prime-time newsmagazine program, "Eye to Eye." And she denied all these stories about abuse, about pressure.

Golden became disgusted with the media. They went overboard, she said, in reporting her seven marriages. And they didn't even call her by her right name, she complained.

"They call me LaVona. That is my legal name, but I didn't even know it was my name until I got married and met my real parents for the first time," she told freelancer Risa Krive. "The name I have always gone by is Sandy. The papers don't even know that.

"They say I've been married at least ten times—that was the last I heard, three days ago. By now I should have at least twelve husbands!" And she laughed.

On January 16, "60 Minutes" broadcast a student film made in 1986, when Harding was sixteen years old, and Golden was particularly upset. The film showed Harding's side of a phone conversation with LaVona. After hanging up, Harding says, "What a bitch!" and tells how her mother berated her for falling on a jump.

Golden says she didn't watch the broadcast. "I told my lawyer to watch the program because I had no intention of watching it. I knew it was not real. It was all fake."

She also said that Harding didn't have it quite as tough as has been reported. "She didn't really have a bad life—she had what a person would classify as normal." Everything except the skating was normal—that required special sacrifices.

Little Tonya got out of nonessential classes in school so she could practice skating, her mother said, and that probably had made other children jealous. And they had to move a lot, so that Tonya could find year-round schooling. The desire and drive to skate all came from Tonya, not her mother, insisted Golden.

"I tried to bribe her out of skating by getting her a horse," Golden recalled. "It took a while, but I found out that skating is a very expensive sport—when we started I didn't realize that. It was very expensive at the beginning—I made all her costumes. But then there were events and competitions that she had to go to out of state, and we had to get there, stay somewhere, and eat—it was terribly expensive. I tried to get her interested in something else, so I got her a pony. She wanted the pony and the skating—so I got rid of the pony."

Harding is fond of saying that she wasn't raised with a silver spoon in her mouth, but Golden says her own girlhood was different from her famous daughter's.

"I had everything handed to me on a silver platter," she said. "I had a baby grand piano, a swimming pool, eleven guest rooms to take my friends home from boarding school." The problem was that the woman who raised her was abusive, LaVona said, as was Golden's first husband. It was all very difficult, Golden complained, "going from wealthy to nothing."

Not that Tonya's life was so bad, her mother emphasizes. Tonya and her other children— much older than Tonya—"always had the best of what I could give them." Golden said she had made sure they had a nice home, nice furniture. Their food, she said, was mostly what they hunted or fished for themselves.

"I made all the children's clothes or bought them from Goodwill, the Salvation Army, St. Vincent de Paul. In fact, Tonya's first pair of skates came from Goodwill. I never bought anything unless it was almost new."

Tonya Harding was only three when she decided she wanted to be an Olympic figure skating champion. During the next two decades, Diane Rawlinson made that dream possible.

The relationship almost didn't happen. When LaVona Harding brought her four-year-old daughter to the Jantzen Beach Arena, where Rawlinson coached several national-class skaters, the former Ice Capades soloist said no, thanks.

"I told them I didn't work with beginners. She should take beginning lessons, and maybe I would work with her in a few years," Rawlinson said.

But Harding's stubborn streak was broad even then.

For a week the child walked on skates—she hadn't learned to glide—around Rawlinson and her elite skaters, and the coach finally gave in. "We were her target and she was going to circle us. I finally decided the only way I could have control over the situation was to be her coach. I said I'd do it on a week-to-week basis."

But a weekly promise became a commitment of years.

Rawlinson saw a child with promise, a rare determination and a crying need for stability. She responded by guiding Tonya on ice and trying to offer support to her off the ice. Harding had great athletic talent. She learned slowly but correctly, the way Rawlinson taught her, so that she could land successful triple jumps at nine—an age when most girls could manage only singles.

Rawlinson brought friends to watch Tonya. One couple saw the little girl doing jumping jacks in the corner of the rink and were entranced. They helped pay for her ice time and coaching.

Rawlinson likes her skaters to be well-rounded, to study their homework, have friends, develop a life outside the rink. Harding did just the opposite. Rawlinson sometimes threw up her hands in frustration— "Coaching Tonya can be an adventure," she said once—but she also saw in Tonya some of her own childhood in Seattle.

"Skating was my whole self-image. When I stepped on the ice, I could be whoever I wanted to be and that's who I wanted to be," Rawlinson said. "Tonya's skating has really been her foundation in life. It's the only thing that has remained a constant."

Rawlinson learned how hard it was to break from that life when a traffic accident in the early 1970s forced her to stop skating. It was two years before she accepted the loss. "I couldn't feel special without my skating. I think I finally grew up."

She saw Harding embrace the skater's life and didn't hesitate to pay for the boots, buy the plane ticket or give of her coaching knowledge to make sure the young skater had every on-ice opportunity she could find.

Even though she cared deeply about Harding, she had less control off the ice.

Tonya was always close to her father, Al. Her stepbrothers and stepsister were much older, not playmates at all, and her father was the bright spot in a lonely childhood. He taught her how to split wood and handle a gun. She killed her first deer at age thirteen, and she was as handy with a wrench as most teen-age girls are with a telephone. But though she could change a set of brake shoes, she never learned how to deal with people. She set her eyes on the prize and blasted ahead. Those in the way had better clear a path.

"She has her own set of rules," said one Portland skating coach. "When she's on the ice, she's the best in the arena and she figures she doesn't have to follow the typical rules, like giving the right of way to other coaches if you're not having a lesson, or waiting your turn to play your program music."

Tonya dropped out of high school, the better to concentrate on her skating. She got a job at a fast-food potato stand in the shopping mall where she practiced. But she never held a real job for long. As she said several years later, skating was her job. It was what she did for twenty years. And she expected a paycheck for all that work—a big paycheck.

When Harding was fifteen years old she had a tumultuous year. She went to the national championships for the first time and finished a strong sixth. Her parents' marriage crumbled for good. She was in an auto accident and badly hurt her back; for a time it looked as if she might never be able to skate again. Slowly but surely, she got back on the ice.

Tonya Harding would blossom into a world-class skater, but she skated with more power than grace. Her body was small and compact, full of fast-twitch fibers. She couldn't create an elegant line with long limbs, but she could carry her speed through her routines and jumps like nobody's business.

John McBride, who owns the Valley Ice Arena in Beaverton, Oregon, has watched Harding for fifteen years. He's seen her land quadruple loops in practice—a jump less than a handful of men even attempt. If Harding lined up in a sprint with a professional hockey team, McBride said, the fastest hockey centers would finish twenty yards in her wake.

"This girl is a Larry Bird or a Wayne Gretzky, a Babe Ruth," McBride insisted. "She's the best there has ever been athletically. There is not another figure skater who has ever laced up skates who could hold her skates. She has more talent than God has ever given anybody."

2

Love and Happiness

Tonya Harding and Jeff Gillooly found each other in 1986. Harding noticed the slender, dark-haired man watching her practice at the Clackamas Town Center. Curious, Harding skated up to the stranger and boldly introduced herself.

Gillooly, just as boldly, asked her out.

Harding was a fifteen-year-old who soon would drop out of high school in her sophomore year. Gillooly, eighteen, was an unexceptional student who had graduated that year from David Douglas High School. She was a figure skater on the rise. He worked at a downtown Portland department store.

Gillooly's early life is almost a blank page. Because he was not an athlete or a musician, his only appearances in his high school yearbooks were class portraits. Gillooly did have an aptitude for business, friends said.

"He was more a talker, and I mean that in a

good way, not a bad one," Gillooly's older brother, Joel, would remember. "But he was more developed in social skills than in athletic skills."

When he met Harding, Gillooly was working at a tailoring shop at the downtown Meier & Frank department store. A few years later, he would go to work filling orders at an Oregon Liquor Control Commission warehouse, a mind-numbing job that paid the bills for almost three years. In a Multnomah County courtroom in 1994, Gillooly described his real job as managing his wife's career, although that often amounted to selling T-shirts to raise money.

On the evening of what was supposed to be their first date, a violent incident occurred. Harding was at home alone, curling her hair and doing the things a teen-age girl does to prepare for a first date. Chris Davison, Tonya's twenty-six-year-old half-brother, came home drunk. He asked Harding for a hug and, when she briefly put her arms around him, he fondled her breast. Harding broke away, but Davison followed, asking her to kiss him. Tonya slapped him and, when that didn't stop him, burned Davison with a curling iron. She then locked herself in a bathroom, emerged, broke away from Davison and called 911.

Davison threatened to kill her if she told anyone he had attacked her. But he wouldn't leave her alone, and she fought him off with a hockey stick. Finally, the police arrived and arrested Davison.

The Clackamas County sheriff's deputies found Harding in tears. When she stopped crying, Harding rejected the deputies' offer to call in medical personnel to check her.

Harding later told her friends that Davison had raped her. He pleaded guilty to resisting arrest in the assault. Two years later, Davison would be killed in a hit-and-run accident. He died when he was struck by a car while walking across a Portland street. An autopsy revealed that he was legally drunk at the time. Detectives never identified the driver, and eventually the investigation was suspended.

(After the Kerrigan attack, there were so many media inquiries about the accident that the police issued a statement: "There is no evidence or reason to believe that Harding or any relatives are associated with, had any involvement or knowledge regarding this accident.")

"He did have a problem with drinking,"

LaVona told *Sports Illustrated* in 1992. "I wouldn't put it past Chris to try and get a kiss. Tonya has a vivid imagination. She has a tendency to tell tall tales." Neither Harding's mother or father had believed her when she told them Davison had attacked her.

Harding's relationship with her mother was steadily falling apart. The marriage of Al and LaVona had broken up after fifteen years. Al had left in search of work and LaVona soon would marry James Golden. Even when Tonya was successful, such as her sixth-place finish in her first national championship, LaVona would criticize and condemn. Tonya took it without tears as a child, but she rebelled as a teen-ager.

Jeff Gillooly would bring a new kind of support to Harding's life. Harding would later describe Jeff as the rock that held her steady and made her life good. She even skated better and, with Jeff at her side, she began climbing through the ranks of national skaters.

There was a trade-off, however, at least as far as her friends were concerned. When Tonya was with Jeff, she ignored her old friends. The year before she met Gillooly,

Harding had grown close to the Webber family. David Webber was the manager of a fast-food restaurant where Harding bought coffee. The skater took to calling David "Dad" and Ruth Webber "Mom." She became best friends with their daughter, Stephanie, and her brothers, Mark and Brent.

As Harding and her own mother grew further apart, she grew closer to the Webbers—but then Gillooly entered her life. In 1988, Jeff and Tonya moved in together. Two years later, on March 18, 1990, they invited a few friends and family members to a chapel in Vancouver, Washington, and were married. Stephanie Webber, who had disapproved of Jeff from the start, was nevertheless the maid of honor. The newlyweds spent their wedding night at a Portland hotel.

Stephanie wasn't the only one who questioned Harding's choice. Neither Al nor LaVona had liked Jeff. Friends of Tonya's thought he tried to control her life and that he would ruin her career.

"I don't know him that well," David Webber later said. "I talked with him several times, and he seemed like a quiet person. But the key thing to know is that we never saw much of Tonya when they were together. We saw a lot of her when they were apart."

And, before the marriage was even two years old, there was violence.

On June 18, 1991, Harding filed for divorce from Gillooly in Polk County, south of Portland. The next day, a circuit court judge in Clackamas County issued a restraining order against Gillooly, prohibiting him from entering Harding's home or any ice rink where she was training or performing.

"He wrenched my arm and wrist and he pulled my hair and shoved me," Harding said in her petition for the restraining order. "I recently found out he bought a shotgun and I am scared for my safety."

The next month, the divorce case was moved to Clackamas County, where Harding and Gillooly were living. Harding wanted the court to award her sole ownership of the couple's prized Bluewater boat. On July 14, Portland police were called when a fight broke out between Harding and Gillooly over the boat at a marina on the Willamette River.

According to Harding, Gillooly's brother John had followed her to the marina, where he contacted Jeff. When Jeff showed up, he

waved an ax handle and shouted at Harding.
Tonya called the police, but before they
arrived, Jeff said, "I think we should break
your legs and end your career." His brother
hopped over a boat trailer and threatened the
terrified skater with a club.

But in a special report filed in addition to
the incident report, Portland police described
a different scene. Gillooly told police that the
boat had been parked on a trailer at his mother's house. When he went outside that July
morning, the boat and trailer were gone.
Gillooly suspected Harding and headed to the
marina where they had bought the boat
because he thought Tonya might try to sell it
there.

When Gillooly found Harding and the boat
in the marina parking lot, an argument broke
out. One of the first officers on the scene
described Harding's reaction to police. "Hi,
I'm Tonya Harding, the world-class skater.
I'm too busy to be having problems like this,
and I've got a restraining order against Jeff."

In mid-August, a Clackamas County judge
ordered Gillooly and Harding to stay away
from each other, and a month later another
judge ordered the boat held in storage so neither Harding or Gillooly could use it.

But Harding's troubles weren't over. On September 3, she called the police when a boyfriend named Shane Mallory entered her apartment and found her with another man. Harding told police Mallory refused to leave, and he wrestled the telephone from her—cutting her finger in the scuffle—when she tried to call for help. Mallory told police he thought he and Harding still had a relationship but that "he would have no problem staying away from Ms. Harding."

Harding soon met another man, a young Canadian, who visited her in October. Her friends and family liked the man, and she seemed calmer around him. But within days, Tonya was telling friends she was back with Jeff. On November 13, Harding asked that the divorce from Gillooly be put on hold so they could work out their differences. They were apparently successful. In February 1992, when she signed the petition to withdraw the divorce, Tonya signed her name "Harding Gillooly."

"I'm a complete person again," Harding told *Sports Illustrated*. "I know it seemed like I was happy, but something was missing, and now I know what it was. Jeff and I love each other more than ever. We're going to get a counselor and work it out. I know he's changed. I see it in his eyes, and I believe in him. I'm going to be married once in my whole life, and that's the way I'm going to look at it. I don't want to lose him. I really don't."

But if Tonya and Jeff had a hard time staying apart, they had a harder time staying together. The trajectory of Tonya and Jeff's romance can be traced in police files. During 1993, their names appeared with numbing regularity, usually with Harding listed as the victim, Gillooly as the suspect.

They had a terrible argument in March. Harding told police Gillooly had grabbed her hair and slammed her head into the bathroom floor next to the toilet. She tried to escape; he chased her in his pickup. She hid between houses to escape. Friends picked her up in the middle of the night and took her home. She was shaken, chunks of her hair were missing or loosened, her hand was red and swollen. She said Gillooly had slammed her fingers in the car door.

She told her friends she was through with her husband, and they believed her. How could anyone take that kind of abuse?

A few days later the police recorded Gillooly's side of the story. "He said he would never hurt his wife," the report says. "He did not hit her or pound her head into the floor." He said that he merely took her by the shoulders to try to calm her down and that he was concerned about her safety, so he followed her in the truck to try to talk her into coming home. It was because he cared about her.

During the next few months, Harding kept calling the cops. She got another restraining order and filed for divorce. In the summer of 1993, Harding complained that Gillooly was following her on the highway. She said he had stolen a leather jacket from her house. She said she had received second-hand death threats from him.

He denied all.

Also that summer, her white 1977 Ford pickup—outfitted with a CD player—was stolen. Tonya was furious. She suspected Gillooly. She told Chris Hayes and Dan Doherty, two men she worked out with at a gym near the rink, that she wanted Gillooly taken care of. They weren't sure what she meant. Harding had approached one of them a few days before about being her bodyguard to protect her from her husband, but now she wanted them to knock Gillooly out of the picture altogether—to kill him.

They were astounded. She said that most people wanted $100,000 for this kind of job because of who she was, famous and all. They laughed it off but had no doubt she was serious. She asked if they wanted to go out with her, take a dip in a hot tub. They declined.

A few days later she amended her offer, said one of the men. She wanted to know if someone would just beat up Gillooly for her— "slap him around a little," he said. The man was offended. He stopped working out with her.

In September, the license plate from Harding's truck was sent to Portland radio station KKRZ-FM. The return address read: "Robin Hood and His Merry Men, Sherwood Forest, Nottingham, England."

Harding did not hesitate to date other men during her separations from Gillooly. But her husband was always there, one way or another.

In the spring of 1993 she dated Tom Arant of Milwaukie, a suburb of Portland. He said it was a short, intense romance, which was unusual for him. He liked to take things slower. But Harding was different; she had a history of brief, dramatic relationships with men and with her friends. She talked a lot about Gillooly, he said, about how she disliked him. About how mean he was to her. And she smoked cigarettes a lot, too, blaming it on stress over her problems with Gillooly. "But she couldn't stop talking to him," Arant said. "If I don't like someone, I don't talk to him. But she had to talk with him at least three or four times a week."

Eventually, perhaps inevitably, she went back to Gillooly.

Wendy Goold has known Harding since before she won her first national championship in 1991. She is not a skater, but they became friends. Like many friends, they resemble each other. They are both petite blondes, with pony-tails and ready smiles. Goold worries about Harding, worries about her a lot.

They lived together twice in 1993, when Harding was separated from her husband. Goold had even introduced Harding to Arant, a good-looking man who she thought would be a good, stable influence. In the spring of

1993, they had all lived together with another friend in a house near Boring, Oregon.

But Harding left the group to go back to Gillooly, then left him once again and returned to Goold. The two friends decided to move into a two-bedroom apartment in Clackamas as roommates.

Goold, who works in an accountant, said she tried to be a good influence, to show Harding that, despite her rough upbringing and her problems with Gillooly, there were alternatives: Kind men, good jobs, a nice life. Stability. But it didn't work. Harding never seemed to appreciate the alternatives.

"I think somewhere in there she's a really good person," Goold said. "I've seen her at her best."

But she didn't understand Harding's attraction to Gillooly. It baffled her. At least once, Goold said, she and Harding were out at McMenamins pub in Milwaukie. Gillooly came in and took away Harding's drink, french fries and cigarettes. "He was very controlling," Goold remembered.

When Harding decided in the summer of 1993 to go back to Gillooly, Goold was disgusted. She would move out of their apartment right after Labor Day.

Although the divorce was already in the works and would be declared final in August, Harding told friends she wanted to "have the divorce annulled," and she and Gillooly continued to call each other husband and wife.

A month later, in early October, Harding also moved out. She left at three o'clock in the morning, putting her things into Gillooly's pickup. It did not go smoothly.

The neighbors heard a loud argument, then a gunshot. Some saw a man pick a woman up off the ground and force her into the cab of the truck. They thought she had been shot.

Police stopped the truck as it was driving away. Inside were Harding, Gillooly, a handgun and a shotgun. A police officer handcuffed the once and future national champion figure skater to the front of his patrol car. He read her the Miranda rights. He talked with Gillooly in the back of his car, then with Harding. They said that the gun had gone off accidentally when Gillooly was carrying it, but their stories didn't match. Finally, the couple admitted that Harding fired the gun, but they didn't want that known. Harding was worried about the publicity.

Gillooly conceded that they had been fighting, about a woman he had been seeing. But he didn't want to press charges.

Nobody but Harding knows why she stuck so long with Gillooly. "The question I always had when I was having problems with Tonya was how much of it was Tonya and how much was Jeff," said Michael Rosenberg, her former sports agent who dissolved their relationship in the fall of 1993. "Because when Jeff was not around, everything seemed to go much smoother," he added.

"I think she loves him and holds on to him and she hates him and is afraid of him."

3

Fire and Ice

The big, difficult jumps must come early in the program, when the skater still has energy. Then it is a matter of hanging on, lasting. In 1991, on a cold February afternoon in Minneapolis, Tonya Harding glided to center ice to begin her long program. She wore a long-sleeved dress the color of Crest toothpaste. She was the decided underdog.

That afternoon Kristi Yamaguchi was supposed to win. After all, she had finished second in this competition the past two years. She had just skated her flowing, artistic program and made only one glaring mistake, falling on a triple lutz. But her scores were good enough for gold.

Almost everyone in the stands and the judges' box at the U.S. Championships expected Harding to fall, too. She always did. She was an "athletic" skater, considered an insult in the skating world and one of the strangest prejudices in sports.

Figure skating ideally combines the best of athletic achievement and balletic movement. But the big jumps often require a big setup by the skater, when the athlete cannot be concerned with flowing arm movements and music synchronization—long seconds when the skater is just poised, coiled, gathering speed for the jump. Tonya Harding was this kind of athlete.

And she kept trying the triple axel, a jump only the best male skaters and only one female, Japan's Midori Ito, had ever landed in competition. Just seven months before, in this same city during the Olympic Festival, Harding had also tried to land this difficult jump. That's all anyone waited for in her program— that big jump. And, as usual, she fell. She finished second then behind the only other really good skater there, Nancy Kerrigan, who tried a low-risk, "artistic" program that took advantage of the elegant lines her long limbs trace.

When Harding fell on her early big jumps, some spectators in the stands would start thumbing through their programs. Without those jumps, she wasn't much to look at.

Harding tried high-risk moves and usually lost the gamble.

But this time in Minneapolis it was different. Harding began her program and landed a triple jump, then stroked to the other end of the ice. There, forty-five seconds after the music started, she braced, swung her leg around and rose in the air. She spun three and a half times and landed solidly on her right skate, her mouth open in astonishment, history made.

Everyone in the crowd knew what had happened. A roar erupted, Harding smiled broadly, waved her hands in triumph, went on with her program with more energy than she had ever felt in her life. Her music was an odd mix of the theme from the movie Batman, "Send in the Clowns" and "Wild Thing." But the crowd was watching, not listening. Harding landed six different triple jumps in all, including a triple-toe, triple-toe combination. Even before the music stopped, 10,000 people were standing, cheering. Harding put her hands to her face, crying and laughing at the same time. Those four minutes of Harding's program, climaxed with that big jump, would remain one of the sport's great moments. In the most predictable of games, Harding had scored a huge upset. Her scores contained another surprise: a perfect 6.0 for technical merit from one judge, the first perfect score any woman had received in such a competition in almost twenty years.

It seemed there was nowhere to go but up. Harding was only twenty years old and on her way. "Tonya is a creature of habit," her coach, Dody Teachman, said after the win. "Once she lands something in competition, she tends to keep doing it."

But that was the last and only time she landed the triple axel and stayed on her feet throughout a program in a major competition. Almost immediately, things started to go sour for Tonya Harding.

During the awards ceremony, the medals got mixed up. Yamaguchi, her eyes red and swollen from crying over her finish, got the silver medal. Nancy Kerrigan, who finished third, got the bronze. But Harding was given the fourth-place medal in the ceremony. The officials just went on with the ceremony, but Harding knew something was wrong right away—the real medal was much bigger and it was gold.

Afterward, at a news conference, Harding answered questions. She was coughing so much the reporters asked if she had a cold. No, she said, I have asthma. They asked about her health, her jumping, her life. When she said she had called her husband in Oregon to tell him about the win, reporters were very interested. It is unusual, in a sport where the athletes are usually so young and so isolated, to find a competitor who had a life outside the rink. The reporters wanted to know about this husband, his job, how long they had been married, what his name was.

"Jeff Gillooly," Harding said, obviously annoyed with all these questions that had nothing to do with skating.

Reporters murmured among themselves. "How do you spell that?" one asked.

"Spell what?" Harding said.

"The last name."

"H-A-R-D-I-N-G," she said, smiling not at all.

Exactly one month later, at the world championships in Munich, Germany, Harding was on the winners' podium again. This time, though, Yamaguchi was wearing the gold medal, Harding the silver. Once again, Harding had nailed a triple axel, but she had botched three other jumps in her program, landing only four triples.

There was a problem with this ceremony, too—a happy problem. The officials were having trouble finding an American flag. They had only two American flags on hand, but that was not enough; they needed three. Another American—Nancy Kerrigan—had finished third. It was a U.S. sweep, the first for any country at the world championships.

It looked like the start of a golden age for U.S. figure skaters. Both Yamaguchi and Kerrigan vowed that they would add triple axel jumps to their repertoires. Japan's Ito had done extremely poorly in Munich, literally falling out of the rink. She was clearly too injured to last much longer at the world level.

The 1992 Olympics were less than a year away for the three top American skaters, and the 1994 Winter Games were only three years away. In 1991, everyone was chasing Tonya Harding's skill level. She was on top. Everything looked shiny bright.

After winning the 1991 U.S. Championships, Tonya Harding, the Cinderella skater, didn't go to the ball. Tom Collins, who produces a

big, prestigious traveling ice show, tradition-
ally stages a huge, fancy party for all the winners of the nationals. But when the party was
in full swing, Harding was spotted elsewhere,
wearing jeans and a sweatshirt, wielding a
cue, playing pool in a hotel bar. In a sport
cloaked in fur and sparkles, Harding has
always stood out. The higher she rose in the
system, the more stark was the figure she cut.

Figure skating is its own small world filled
with fiercely loyal devotees. People who can
tell a triple loop from a triple lutz are few and
far between. The knowledge is specialized
and the skills developed over a long period of
time, with regimented, lonely training routines. There are many written rules in figure
skating, and just as many unwritten ones.

Elite figure skaters are rarely friends in any
sense of the word. They usually train in different parts of the country and meet at skating
events two or three times a year.

The women are especially competitive. The
ladies' championship is the crown jewel of
the sport and they know it. They don't talk to
each other in practice, concentrating instead
on their coaches and their work. Sometimes,

they skate dangerously close to each other, not entirely by accident. French skater Surya Bonaly caused a small uproar in 1992 when she performed "in your face" backflips—a move banned in competition—when she was on practice ice with her competitors.

Harding is no exception, except that she may be even more competitive. And she talks about it, in front of microphones, breaking another of her sport's unwritten rules. Harding refuses to follow many rules. And she has always had trouble maintaining the illusion of decorous femininity that has long been seen as synonymous with the sport.

"There is more pressure on females, a stigma to be pretty and glamorous on the ice," said Elizabeth Manley, the silver medalist at the 1988 Calgary Games. "Tonya is not in that category. She is fast and a little bit more bullish going into her jumps. ... That's what makes her different, entertaining. She is a fireball on the ice, not a princess."

Figure skating is all about illusion. Nothing is what it seems. The competitors perform difficult, athletic feats but smile through pain and disappointment. They must never sweat. Makeup brightens their cheeks, their eyes, covers the nightmare bruises on their legs.

The women's costumes rely heavily on flesh-colored net, which helps to emphasize a performer's apparently partial nudity. The athletes should appear to be spangled with wisps of ethereal sparkle and heavenly fabric.

And when the skaters fall, come crashing down, they must immediately pick themselves up and move their arms to the music and smile and go on as if nothing happened. Everything is fine. And when it is over and the winners stand on the podium, they hug each other, kiss the air beside each other's ears. The best of friends. There are no microphones or reporters near, which is fine, because they usually have nothing to say to each other. Nothing at all.

All sports are subjectively judged, one way or another. A home-plate umpire must call balls and strikes. The football referee uses his judgment to decide whether a catch was inbounds, a player offside, whether there was interference. In any organized sport someone, somewhere, determines whether the rules have been followed properly. And these subjective decisions can and do determine who wins and who loses.

Some sports rely more heavily on human judgment than others, of course. And gymnastics, diving, synchronized swimming and figure skating, sports that are subjectively judged, often draw harsh criticism from sports "purists."

It's silly, they say. It's unfair. It's not a "real" sport.

The men who say this (they are, inevitably, men) do not criticize Olympic boxing and wrestling, sports that also rely on judging for scores; and they almost never truly understand the sport they are griping about. But then, few people understand figure skating.

The most athletic thing about the sport is the jumps, but to the untrained eye they are virtually impossible to tell apart. The differences between lutzes, loop and flip jumps are minute, insignificant to almost anyone who hasn't been trained as a skater. They all depend on whether a skater's inside or outside edge or toe pick has been used, what the skater's body looks like going into the jump or upon landing.

In the press section at competitions, the reporters, even veteran Olympic writers, try to sit near figure skating coaches or former skaters turned journalists. These people can

identify the jumps and call them out when—
and if—they occur.

"What was that?" is a common question in
the press area.

"Did she make it?" is another. That's
because sometimes, even if a skater stays on
her feet, she may not have technically "landed" a jump. She could have "two-footed" it,
instead of landing on just one skate, which
means the jump doesn't count. Or taken an
extra step between the two jumps that form a
combination, which also is a deduction.
These crucial distinctions can be tough to see
and tough to judge.

"What color would you call that?" is another question that is often heard. Reporters note
the hue of the costumes and their sequins, the
musical accompaniment, and the mood of the
performer's gestures. Not the usual sports
reporting—but part of the sport of figure skating. How the athlete looks and responds to
music is part of the scoring, part of the rules
of the game.

All of this is outlined in fat rule books that
the judges must be intimately familiar with.
At the top levels of skating, the judges are all
seasoned and experienced. They know what
to look for, can see the minute mistakes made

at top speed that the audience sometimes misses. And they know more than the spectator at a single event could ever see.

That is what bothers the sport's critics the most—those scores that seem to come from nowhere, that seem to come from judges who made up their minds before the competition. And there's every possibility that sometimes that is indeed the case. Judges go to practice, and what skaters do in practice counts toward their final scores, consciously or not. The judges want to see the skaters perform their routines so they will know what to expect, so they won't be surprised, so they know when to pay attention, and to what. They do this so they can make more informed decisions about a skater's performance. But the skaters are not stupid. They know that if they look neat and stylish on the ice at all times, the judges will look on them more favorably. So practice at competitions is very much a fashion show. And the skaters know that their personal comportment is important. This is a sport that likes to maintain a wholesome image, and one where the athletes are usually very young and managed by people who are much older.

Having judges at practice may strike many people like an ethical violation, a compromise of their ability to remain impartial. But it has a compelling sort of logic. If a skater lands a difficult jump consistently in practice and has landed it in other events, judges may well be inclined to view a fall on the same jump, during competition, in a more favorable light. After all, the skater can do it and shouldn't be too heavily penalized for trying. On the other hand, if the skater can't do a jump, has never successfully landed a jump, and yet tries it during competition, a judge is likely to roll her eyes and mark a fall with a sterner hand.

That is one reason why, in figure skating, "paying your dues" is all part of competition. Skaters know that when they are up-and-coming, they may see the older champions getting breaks at their expense. But if they stick around long enough, they will see the breaks go their way.

The skaters' coaches know that the judges are all powerful and they do not complain, except very rarely or off the record, about marks. And the smartest coaches cultivate the judges—seek their advice on their skaters' performances, music, and costumes. Some judges do not hesitate to let coaches know what their skaters are doing wrong and suggest remedies or improvements. It is another way the sport keeps moving, behind the scenes, just as much a part of the action as trades or deals in baseball. There are politics, of course, but those politics often cut both ways—Tonya Harding, like most skaters, has been both a victim and a beneficiary of judging politics.

But unlike most skaters—unlike any other skater, in fact—she almost totally controls her own destiny. She is the only woman who can do a triple axel, the most difficult and easily recognizable of the triple jumps. If Harding skates a clean program and includes her big jump, she wins, period. No judge, no matter how much he or she may dislike Harding's costumes or lifestyle, can deny her. No other skater can match that level of difficulty. Harding, with her athletic ability, makes figure skating more of a "pure" sport.

Perhaps the most appealing aspect of sports is the unambiguous character of it all. There are rules, there are boundaries, there are points. You do or you don't. You win or you lose. The races go to the swiftest, the contests to the strongest. Things are fair. Sport is an escape from real life, which is, as we all know, messy and uncertain.

Figure skating is often criticized for being absurd and unreal. A little fantasy world. But this is exactly wrong. In skating, looks count. Reputation counts. Performance counts, but allowances can be made. More than any other sport, figure skating is like real life

4

The Harder They Fall

Most skaters take only one serious run at an Olympic medal. The training regimen of an elite skater is too long, too hard, too boring. The money is too tight; the scent of fast bucks made with a traveling ice show is too alluring. One Olympics is all they want, all they have time for.

But not Tonya Harding. Because of the International Olympic Committee's decision to stop holding the Summer and Winter Games in the same year, an "extra" Winter Olympics was added to the schedule, to be held just two years after the conclusion of the Games in 1992. Tonya now had two Games to focus on—when she would be twenty-one and twenty-three years old—prime ages for a skater.

Curiously, after her triumph at the 1991 national championships and her silver-medal performance at the world championships,

Harding seemed to slack off in her training. She didn't intensify her efforts, as did Kristi Yamaguchi and Nancy Kerrigan. Yamaguchi trained in Edmonton, Alberta, and lived with her coach. Far from her home in Northern California, the world champion ran through her new Olympic-year programs almost daily, honing every move, striving for perfection.

Meanwhile, Harding lived at home, in Portland, and had a rocky year with her new husband. In June 1991 she filed for divorce from Gillooly and asked for a restraining order to keep him away from her. She would skate well some days, badly on others—and sometimes not show up for training at all. And she had trouble with her coaches. She fired Dody Teachman as her coach in April 1991 and briefly reunited with her former coach, Diane Rawlinson, before going back to Teachman yet again.

Her marriage was on again, off again. A writer from *Sports Illustrated* came to Portland to do a long feature story about Harding—a sure sign that she had arrived as a major athlete. But she was an athlete with a most interesting story to tell—and she told it, sparing little detail. The assault by the now-dead half-brother, the poverty of childhood, the strained relationship with her coaches and mother, the marital storms. And she posed for pictures with a new man in her life, her new boyfriend, her new love. There she was, she seemed to be saying, take her or leave her.

But her overwhelming talent was still there, still dominant, and in September, at a Skate America International competition, she won, beating Yamaguchi. In October she reunited with Gillooly. Once again, things looked to be on the upswing.

But by winter, with the pressure growing, Harding's troubles became harder to hide. She was overweight, out of shape. Her training was, at best, sporadic. The magazine's fact checkers went over the story with her and discovered that she was back again with her husband—photographs had to be reshot for the article and the ending had to be redone. Gillooly declined to be interviewed.

In early January 1992, the *Sports Illustrated* story came out, entitled "Not Your Average Ice Queen." It was largely sympathetic to Harding—the basic slant was the old story of a tough cookie who had surmounted incredible odds to succeed in her sport, the basic American dream. While virtually all the information in the story had come from Harding herself, she was devastated. She felt as if her life had been been exposed like an open sore, and she was worried about the effect the story would have on the prim figure skating judges.

The article came out just before the national championships and Olympic trials in Orlando, Florida. Harding, as is customary, had a news conference before she began her competition. But this time she had to do it the day after a major story which she considered a huge embarrassment.

Harding told reporters she didn't like some of the elements in the story but declined to be more specific.

Was the story accurate?

"In parts," Harding said.

Was she pleased with it?

"In parts," she replied.

When pressed further she said, "It's fine. I'm here to talk about my skating. I think everything is going real positive for me. I'm happy. There are a few things that can be said about the article, but there's not any reason to. It's only an article."

The news conference moved on to mostly talking about her skating. Afterward, coach Dody Teachman said, "This could have been a real nightmare, but I think it went quite well."

Harding was also relieved. She had been nervous beforehand, she told *Oregonian* writer Terry Richard, and she had help from her coaches. "They talked to me and I listened," Harding said. "But I basically went in there and did what I wanted to do."

She said her main regret about the magazine's story was that "they never put in there that my husband has been really supportive of me." She thought that was important, even though at the time she talked to the writer, she was separated from Gillooly and was dating other men.

"Jeff always put food on the table and a roof over my head," Harding told Richard. "He paid for my skating for a couple of years. If it hadn't been for him during that time, I wouldn't have been skating. I don't think he looked very good in the article. But there's no problem between us."

Questions about her personal life taken care of, Harding got ready to defend her national title and earn a spot on the Olympic team, which was, of course, her lifelong dream. This was her moment. And then she went out and skated abysmally.

A skater's short or original program is usually more nerve-racking than the long program. There is more pressure to be perfect. Although the short program is worth only one third of a skater's final score, it provides the judges with that all-important first impression. Anyone who falls in the early part of a short program can forget about winning the overall competition.

In Orlando Arena that day, Harding was the sixteenth skater to take the ice. Kerrigan, who was the second skater, had performed a clean program and completed all her required elements, giving her scores of mostly 5.7 (out of a possible 6.0). Those were the numbers to beat.

No other skater had come close to Kerrigan when Harding had her turn. During warmups she landed a big triple axel jump. But when the music began and the judges watched intently, Harding faltered. She went up for her big jump and landed on her rear. Because the triple axel was part of a combination, she was doubly penalized.

Harding blamed an ankle strain from that morning's practice. "When I landed, my foot just buckled under me," she said. "It was very painful." But she said she still planned to try the triple axel in her long program.

After Harding, the reliably brilliant Yamaguchi came out and, as usual, skated beautifully. So going into the long program, the defending champion was only third. And Harding had been given something of a break by the judges—her scores for required elements were all 5.3 or 5.2, but scores for presentation were 5.8 and 5.7s.

In the long program things were no different. Harding took the ice immediately after Yamaguchi's performance, one of the best of her career. Harding was warming up as Yamaguchi's scores for artistic merit were announced—and they included a perfect 6.0, the only one in the competition. The crowd roared.

As the applause quieted, Harding took center ice and waited for her music. Once again she tried the triple axel, and once again came crashing down on her rump. The rest of the four-minute performance was mediocre at best; Harding completed only two triples in all. She limped off the ice.

The judges were more than generous in giving Harding third place and thus a berth on the Olympic team. And Harding tried not to use her sore ankle as an excuse. "It disrupted pleased that I'm on the team and I really don't care whether I'm in first, second or third."

Nancy Kerrigan and Kristi Yamaguchi arrived in Albertville, France, in time for the opening ceremonies for the 1992 Olympic Games. They wore their team uniforms, waved flags and marched, were roommates in the athletes' village, watched other athletes compete. There they were, in the stands, cheering Paul Wylie to a silver medal in the men's figure skating competition. Good friends, good sports. Practicing a few hours a day and just waiting for their chance to compete.

Tonya Harding stayed in Portland. She was nursing her sore ankle and her injured pride after the dismal showing at the nationals. And she had a new excuse—her problems were caused by new skating boots she wore in Orlando. They were too stiff. Harding went back to wearing her old boots.

She practiced in the morning at the shopping mall rink and in the evenings as well. And she decided not to go to France until the last possible minute.

Dody Teachman said that she was practicing well, even as the Olympics were under way. She was skating great, she said. She had lost weight, and she was skating without stopping and restarting, her usual mode of practice.

It wasn't until three days before the women's competition began that Harding got on a plane. Jeff Gillooly walked his wife through the Portland airport, and it was clear that they were annoyed with the reporters and cameras. Gillooly shielded Harding's face with his hands, to spoil pictures. She was a champion athlete on the way to the Olympics. She looked like a criminal on the way to prison.

Clearly, very clearly, something was dreadfully wrong with Harding throughout this period, but she hasn't talked much about it publicly. She said only that it wasn't her fault—her leg was hurt, the boots not right, her asthma had acted up, her coaches were wrong.

After she finally arrived in France, ten days into the Games, she held a press conference.

"Things are going positive for me," she said. "I'm skating good. Yes, I lost weight. The reason I came in late was that I wanted to have the ice time that was available to me at home that would not be available to me here.

I also had won an event, the Oregon Athlete of the Year award. I was supposed to go to the banquet but was not able to go because of fixing boots."

She also said she felt good—like the way she did before the 1991 nationals. She also declared that she had never had jet lag in her life.

- To no one's surprise, Harding fell while trying the triple axel in the Olympic Games. Less than a minute into her original program, she coiled and sprang for the big jump, and crashed. Once again, she was penalized for missing her combination. Midori Ito, favored for the gold but hurting from injuries, decided not to try her triple axel after watching Harding fail. But Ito crashed on a usually reliable—for her—triple lutz.

After the competition, Harding refused to speak to reporters.

She was sixth going into the finals, virtually out of medal contention. After practice the next day, she talked about pulling out all the stops and going for a quadruple loop jump in the free skate, which would have made history. But when it was time to skate for the medals, she tried, once again, to land a triple axel. And once again she fell.

After that shaky start she doubled two other planned triple jumps but ended up landing five double jumps cleanly. It was a solid, if unspectacular, performance, and the judges didn't know quite what to make of it. Her scores for technical merit ranged from 5.3 to 5.7; for artistic impression, from 5.2 to 5.7.

But it was a year when everyone fell. Even Yamaguchi, the eventual gold medalist, hit the ice during the freestyle skate. Midori Ito also attempted a triple axel and fell—but then threw in another later in her program and landed it. The spirited effort vaulted her to a silver medal. And graceful Nancy Kerrigan, in a beautiful white designer costume, was the surprise bronze medalist, despite taking her own inelegant tumble.

If Harding had not tried the triple axel and had stayed on her feet, she would have taken home an Olympic medal. As it was, she finished fourth—no doubt the most frustrating place to finish at an Olympics—and once again refused to talk to reporters. She left France before the closing ceremonies.

Harding came back to Portland and greeted the cameras that were waiting for her at the airport with a sour expression.

"I can't believe you guys are here," she said.

"I didn't tell anyone."

Harding was chafing and ready to make some changes. She dumped her coach, Dody Teachman, and rehired Diane Rawlinson. She fired her choreographer, Barbara Flowers, and hired Erika Bakacs. She decided to do two entirely new programs for the world championships, which were just a month after the Olympics.

One morning in early March, Harding made the news again. Police were called to an intersection in Clackamas County, southeast of downtown Portland. Harding was having an argument with another driver, a woman. When police arrived, they found Harding standing in the street, armed with a baseball bat. Apparently, Harding was in a hurry. She was upset because the car in front of her did not turn right on a red light. Two days later, Harding apologized through her agent, saying that "while it wasn't her fault, she regrets the incident and is sorry that it happened."

When Harding arrived at the world championships, in Oakland, California, nine days later, she faced questions about the incident.

"That was blown way out of proportion; I

feel really sorry about it," she said. "I've learned that people look at me as a celebrity. Sometimes I don't remember that. I don't look at myself as a celebrity." She talked about all the changes in her coaching and programs and said that she would like one more change: from now on she was to be known as Tonya Harding-Gillooly.

Then she went out and skated indifferently. She finished sixth overall, a placing that other skaters' coaches complained about. They were sure Harding had received preferential treatment from the judges.

"There was a game of placements," said Gilles Beyer, who coached skater Laetitia Hubert of France. "We are in the United States and they want to support Harding."

"The judging was horrible," said Nancy Kerrigan's coach, Mary Scotvold. "Hubert was third. I would have been happy with fifth for Nancy, but not if it was behind Harding."

Kerrigan ended up with the bronze, Yamaguchi the gold. The quiet Olympic champ serenely skated away into professional ranks with her *Newsweek* and *Sports Illustrated* covers, her endorsement contracts, her Wheaties box, her medals, and declined to try another Olympics. Meanwhile, Kerrigan and

Harding announced that they would aim for 1994, that they would both go for the gold.

A year and a half later, Harding passionately would insist that she had lost her national title and the 1992 Olympics because of the profile of her that had appeared in *Sports Illustrated*. It had influenced the judges against her, she was sure. They were prejudiced and wouldn't let her win. She told anyone who would listen that everything in the story was "a lie." Everything. The only thing they had gotten right was the spelling of her name.

5

The Hard Luck Club

After 1992, Kristi Yamaguchi swore off the rigors of amateur skating. The professional circuit, with its long days of travel but good pay and easy competition, was what the Olympic and world champion wanted now. Her transition was expected, and so was the ascent of Nancy Kerrigan to fill her spot as America's top amateur skater.

Tonya Harding couldn't control the inevitable. Her poor showing at the 1992 world championships knocked her from her perch near the top of the skating hierarchy. She was back down with the newcomers and developing skaters, assigned to the Skate Canada International for her fall competition instead of one of the more prestigious events. In Victoria, British Columbia, Harding skated against inferior skaters and bombed. She finished fourth, coughing and gasping for air because the cold air triggered an asthma attack.

At the first United States Figure Skating Association-sponsored pro-am event later that fall, Harding finished second to Kerrigan, but the disappointment was eased by the paycheck for $20,000.

But Harding returned to the practice rink with the realization that her asthma was worse. It was harder to get through her long programs and she had to pause in practices to use her inhaler.

Harding is one of nearly ten million Americans who suffer from asthma. Asthma— Greek for "panting"—causes inflammation in the lungs, which makes the lungs produce mucus and contracts the muscles around the airways. A person suffering an asthma attack struggles for breath. The difficulty in getting oxygen varies from person to person, but it can be dangerous enough to lead to death. Some people have mild attacks only when they exercise. For others, it's a daily ordeal.

Tonya Harding was in the second group. She was born with the affliction. When she exercised hard, or when the air was cold and dry, or if a certain kind of pollen was in the air, Harding felt her lungs seize up. An inhaler helped, but the condition had begun affecting her in competition. In Minneapolis in 1991, reporters asked if she had a cold when she couldn't stop coughing. No, just mild asthma, she replied. By Skate Canada in late 1992, Harding felt the condition steal some of her energy in the long program.

Other athletes have competed, and excelled, with asthma. Jackie Joyner Kersee, for example, learned to control the condition and eventually won two Olympic gold medals in the demanding heptathlon. Tonya's friends had been after her for years to see a specialist and to stop relying on over-the-counter medication that didn't always work. In the fall of 1992, the always obstinate Harding finally agreed.

Dr. Marilyn Rudin, a Portland pulmonary specialist, tested Harding's lung capacity. When she was exercising, the skater had use of as little as twenty percent of her capacity. For most of her life, and all of her adulthood, Harding hadn't known what it felt like to draw a normal breath.

The commonly used bronchial dilaters that Harding had relied on treated only the symptoms and often made them worse. The dilaters open air passages by relaxing the muscles controlling the lungs, but they do nothing to help the inflammation that is the main problem. Instead, the inflammation becomes worse when sufferers, trying to get relief, take inhalers more frequently. Studies show that long-term, heavy use can lead to death.

The best treatment, experts agree, is to reduce the swelling—typically using high doses of cortisone—and then begin a regular therapy of cortisone, anti-inflammatories and bronchial dilators to keep the symptoms to a minimum.

That's what Rudin wanted to do for Harding, but she would have to wait until after the national championships. In the meantime, Harding was using a new type of medication, which kept the asthma in check and boosted her energy level.

"I woke up this morning ready to go," Harding said after an on-ice practice. "The only problem is getting too excited. I can feel my heart beating."

With the asthma under control, Harding was able to focus on her programs and the upcoming 1993 national championships in Phoenix, Arizona, where she was expected to be one of three women to earn a trip to the World Championships in Prague. She planned to do the triple axel in her long program and had been hitting the jump consistently in practice until the week before she left Portland. Missing the jump didn't worry her. It would be there when she needed it, she said.

After finishing second at the 1992 championships, Nancy Kerrigan was expected to make the logical step up to champion in Phoenix. Kerrigan didn't willingly accept the role of favorite.

"When I'm on the ice, I just have to concentrate on the skating and what I've been training at home to do," she said. "Out there, in the practices, I'm not really paying attention to the other skaters because I'm doing my own thing, and I have to get ready."

Harding missed her press conference and showed up late for a rescheduled meeting with reporters the next day. She smiled, but she also refused to answer questions about her childhood, personal problems that affected her past performances, and recent weight loss.

"My skating is me and what I like to do and what I want to do," she said. "It really doesn't matter whether I had a blue-collar background or whether I was born with a silver spoon in my mouth. My skating is happy. My life is happy."

Harding stayed happy at the press conference until her coach, Diane Rawlinson, let
slip that the skater had lost the weight using
Jenny Craig's diet plan. Harding glared at her
coach, and stalked out of the room. "Oh,
dear," Rawlinson said with a sigh.

Nancy Kerrigan began her appointed glide
toward the national title by finishing first in
the technical program, but it was Harding
who won over the crowd of almost ten thousand at Phoenix's America West Arena. Kerrigan was all elegance in a black costume;
Harding turned what could have been a skating tragedy into a good laugh and a strong
performance.

She wore a tiny red spangled costume of her
own design for the short program. The sleeveless bodice was caught by a small clasp
behind Harding's neck, and the effect of the
sequins climbing from the material was of
bright flames. Skating second-to-last, Harding began her program to music from the
movie *Footloose*. She spun into the air for her
opening jump, a planned triple lutz-double
toe jump combination, but threw one leg out

and turned the jump into a single at the same time that she clasped her hands to her throat. The arena went silent. The crowd couldn't see what Rawlinson saw.

"As soon as Tonya did her first two moves, I thought, 'Oh, my God, her dress is undone. This should be an interesting lutz,' " Rawlinson recalled.

Pretty soon the crowd was in on the predicament, and Harding shared their laughter. The competition referees let her fix the dress with a safety pin and begin again. Harding hit her opening jump combination as if nothing had happened. With the crowd behind her, she skated a nearly flawless performance, finishing slightly behind Kerrigan going into the long program but within easy range to win.

On the eve of the long program, Harding was up all night. The dry Arizona air and the frigid skating rink had combined to aggravate her asthma. She couldn't stop coughing. The next day, she was exhausted and her skating showed it.

To conserve her energy, Harding skated only a brief warmup. She and Rawlinson already had thrown out the triple axel. She didn't have the strength for that demanding move. Harding hit her opening triple salchow and a double axel-double toe combination, but she looked dispirited and on her next jump, a double lutz, she almost missed the landing. She crashed to the ice on a triple toe loop. With almost ten thousand fans cheering wildly in support of her, Harding left the ice without a smile.

Still, her marks were strong enough to give Harding the lead with four skaters remaining. It appeared that her position on the world team was safe—and that she would win a bronze medal at least—as Nicole Bobek and Tonia Kwiatkowski fell short with the judges. But after Lisa Ervin skated into first with the only clean program of the night among the leaders, and Kerrigan prepared to skate, the leader board changed and Harding dropped to third and, later, to fourth.

Kwiatkowski, an Ohio college student, was moved into third place. Kerrigan took first, despite a pratfall on the ice, and Ervin was second.

"The thing that was really hard was they showed Tonya in first place until the last two skaters," said Rawlinson, who broke the news to the skater. "We're disappointed. Tonya has just excelled in so many ways. She's come so far in her skating, in her attitude."

Harding, Ervin, and Bobek all received some second-place marks. Ervin hit three triple jumps. Harding and Bobek each had two. Kwiatkowski completed only one.

Many of Harding's supporters, and quite a few of the fans at America West Arena that night, felt that Harding was unfairly judged. They pointed out that Kwiatkowski had to put her hand on the ice to steady herself once and then fell on an easier jump than the one Harding missed. The judges were against Harding, they said.

Harding was named first alternate to the world championship team, but she didn't go to Prague. The U.S. team probably could have used her. Kwiatkowski didn't make it out of the qualifying round. Ervin was thirteenth. Kerrigan, the world heir apparent, skated a dreadful long program and was heard crying, "I wish I was dead," when she fell into fifth place.

In early February 1993, Elaine Stamm wrote a letter to The *Oregonian's* new sports columnist, Julie Vader. She had read recent columns and articles about Tonya Harding's performance at the 1993 national championships and felt sorry for the skater.

"We have big hearts, and we love a champion-in-the-making," she wrote. "Here is a bona fide one. . . a plucky, strawberry-blond with an intense love of skating. I'd like to see a Tonya Harding Gillooly Fan Club started, with members supporting her with cards, letters and contributions toward her expenses. . . Could you mention this idea in your column?"

Parts of Stamm's letter were reprinted in *The Oregonian*, and it was enough to get a fan club rolling. The first meeting was on the last day in February; twenty-six people joined. By June, Stamm was able to report that the club had performed several services for Harding. They were listed in *The Skater*, the club's official newsletter:

1. Purchased and hung a large banner on the side of the skating rink (Ice Capades Chalet) where she trains, reading "Home of Tonya Harding—U.S. National Champion, World Silver Medalist, Olympian."

2. Hung a large framed, color photo of Tonya in the rink's skating apparel shop.

3. Obtained speaking engagements for her with Rotary International (she charms them with her personality and it's excellent public

relations).

4. Nominated her for grand marshal of the Troutdale (Oregon) Parade, the city being excited to get her.

5. Given her small monetary gifts to help with expenses.

6. Regularly sent out news releases to the media.

7. Placed framed pictures in the nicest sports bars in Portland (alongside the Trail Blazers!).

8. Kept up a photo/news album.

9. Helped her with phone calls, letters, errands, etc.

10. Arranged with Pay Less Drugs (through them and the USFSA) for them to underwrite her medication.

11. Arranged her appearance before a local middle school assembly, so she could present the students with the Fan Club's donation to the school's "penny drive" for new equipment."

Harding's fan club was clearly not a group that wanted to remain removed. They would come to know their star very well indeed.

Dues for membership ranged from twenty-five dollars, for a "business" membership, to ten dollars for adults to one dollar for those under seven years ("Tots for Tonya"). A member would get a TONYA! bumper sticker, a photo button, a membership card and the newsletter every month. But if fans wanted to show their support even further, they were urged to contribute on the membership application:

"I can further support TONYA by: Making phone calls; Sending TONYA encouraging cards; Bringing more people to meetings; Writing letters to editors; Calling sports talk programs; Donations of money; Free photocopying; Film for Club snapshots; Cosmetics; Hair care; Nail care; Clothing."

The tone of the newsletter was cheerful and chirpy, filled with exclamation points and upbeat news about Harding. There were reports of her new skating programs, costumes and music, new hairstyles, interviews on local radio programs. It was all very positive—at first.

But the tone of *The Skater* began to change. The newsletter editor, Joe Haran, had been a longtime fan of Harding's and a longtime dedicated writer of letters to the editors of local newspapers. He described himself as a Vietnam veteran suffering from post-traumatic stress syndrome, and as someone who identified closely with Harding because of his own childhood of abuse and poverty.

He saw enemies to Harding in the media, the skating "establishment," in other skaters. He thought Harding was badly mistreated by *The Oregonian* when it printed pictures of her falling down and that she was ignored by Portland's TV and radio reporters. Even before the fan club's founding, he had written long letters raging against these injustices. He wrote to skating officials, complaining about the unfair politics of the sport and how they hurt Tonya Harding.

Then, with *The Skater* to edit, he could cheer Harding and poke at her enemies at the same time. In June 1993, he even enlisted Jonathan Swift in Harding's cause, quoting the famous satirist as having said: "When a true genius appears in the world, you may know him by this sign: that the dunces are all in confederacy against him."

Haran, who had for years been a fan who kept his distance from Harding, moved closer and closer. Harding, he later said, began to give him clothes and food and persuaded her father, Al Harding, to let Haran move in with him. It was more evidence of her good and kind nature, he felt.

But Tonya told friends that Haran gave her the creeps, he was so worshipful. Still, she didn't banish him from her circle.

Haran was incensed when Vader published a column in The *Oregonian* about Harding's divorce and turbulent summer. It was a largely sympathetic story, but the writer had seen Harding in a bowling alley one night, smoking cigarettes, and wrote about that as well. Harding had always complained of asthma attacks, and smoking was about the worst habit an asthmatic athlete could have.

Haran wrote an angry letter about the column, claiming that Harding was a battered wife and blameless. Once again, he insisted, the press was out to get his favorite skater.

In October, at the Skate America meet in Dallas, Harding held a pre-competition news conference. She complained about lack of funding. She said she had to wear the same old clothes all the time and it was getting embarrassing. In the past year she'd gotten only $10,000 for training—not nearly enough.

Kristin Matta, an official of the U.S. Figure Skating Association, listened in the back of the room, clearly perturbed. After Harding excused herself, Matta looked through the files and let the reporters know: The skater had received at least $40,000 in training money in the past year, not including the $10,000 Harding had talked about.

The next day, in a press conference after her short program, Phil Hersh of the *Chicago Tribune* asked Harding about the apparent discrepancy. She explained that she counts her years as beginning and ending with the world championships—and that she'd only gotten $10,000 since last March.

It was a confusing answer—reporters immediately dubbed it the "Harding Fiscal Year"—and unsatisfactory.

When *The Oregonian* reported this exchange—in a column about the media's hard time dealing with Harding and vice versa—Haran was angry all over again.

Early in the morning he called Vader's voice mail at *The Oregonian* and left a rambling five-minute message. He was upset. He said unkind things about other figure skaters, including Kerrigan. He called Hersh a "lowlife Nazi." He said Vader was "on a parallel with Joseph Goebbels," made other personal insults, and said, ominously, "One of these days you'll pay for all this" and "I hope someday you're in a lot of pain and hurt."

Ten days later, Harding herself received a death threat when she was scheduled to skate in a low-level event at the Clackamas Town Center.

The November 1993 issue of the Tonya Harding Fan Club newsletter was dedicated almost exclusively to reporting the death threat. Three pages of Haran's breathless prose emphasized how the skater "bore herself with dignity throughout" although there were "several days of anguish, pain, stress and soul-searching for Tonya—days when moral support was forthcoming for her, days when rumors were taken as fact, when otherwise intelligent people succumbed to mendacity, when Tonya's drive and determination overcame her fears and an exhibition at a shopping mall became a testimony to Tonya's force of will and courage: the will and courage to remain in charge of her own life rather than react to a hateful person's sick mind." The anonymous, threatening caller was described as "demented."

The next month's newsletter, focusing on the upcoming national championships, took an even darker, more wounded tone. "SKATING CROWNS KERRIGAN," one article was headlined, and it complained that the national champion was featured on the cover of the official magazine of the U.S. Figure Skating Association: "Gee, we thought Tonya was going for the gold, too! (Tonya's the only U.S. skater to defeat the world champion.) Hmmm. The timing of the cover, on the eve of the Nationals, is a powerful message indeed."

Haran was wrong: Harding had never finished in front of the current world champion, Oksana Baiul of Ukraine.

"TONYA 'EASY TO BEAT' SAYS KERRIGAN" was another headline, which was an inaccurate representation of rather mild comments Kerrigan had made after a recent competition. "That's quite a statement," Haran's article said, "coming as it does from someone who has been protected from competing against Tonya. . . . Perhaps Kerrigan can defeat Tonya in accounting rooms at tournaments, with media favoritism and Eastern Seaboard hype, but she will never defeat Tonya on the ice, at figure skating!"

Another item in this same newsletter was headlined: "PRO-AM SNUBS TONYA." It complained that Harding was not invited to a pro-am tournament, even though at a pro-am tournament in 1992 "Tonya outskated everyone but had to settle for second place."

And yet another article: "TONYA GYPPED IN JAPAN." "The recent NHK Trophy tournament in Chiba, Japan, saw our friend Tonya ambushed by inexperience—the inexperience of three judges who, unlike their counterparts who'd placed Tonya at or near the top, didn't seem to know what they were looking at and placed Tonya in seventh place in the technical program!"

The tone of Haran's newsletter had gone from cheering to griping. Even a little poem for Harding, a fan club newsletter staple, ended on a defensive note:

So when you're on Olympic ice,
Don't let them get you down:
Show those judges and those fans —
That night, you'll *own the town!*

But perhaps the most alarming items were in the November issue—the special "death threat" issue. *The Skater* noted that George Steinbrenner had agreed to underwrite some of Harding's training costs after the death threat. (He did in fact contribute $20,000.)

And the President's Message column written by Elaine Stamm reported: "Someone recently told Tonya a prerequisite for his firm's supporting Tonya was that she '. . . forget the Fan Club.' She refused, primarily because our 'being there' is more important to her than financial aid."

Harding, who had always complained about lack of funding, had apparently chosen these fans over more money, and they were very grateful.

The fan club had set Harding up as the grand marshal of a parade in the little town of Troutdale, Oregon, in the summer of 1993, and after she won her national championship in January 1994, the Troutdale City Council decided to commend her with a special proclamation. Mayor Paul Thalhofer was blissfully unaware of the controversy that would quickly engulf the skater. The Tuesday night after Harding's win, Mayor Thalhofer read a grand proclamation naming Harding "The First Lady of Troutdale."

A few hours later, he learned that Harding was under suspicion of having been involved in the attack on Nancy Kerrigan. "I got home that night and watched the news and said, 'Oh, shit,'" the mayor said. "I stuck both feet into it."

But all this was in the future. First, Tonya would have to survive the 1993 World Championships. Never before had she felt so much unrelenting pressure to succeed.

6

Rough Skating

Tonya Harding needed strong performances if she was to convince her many skeptics that she had what it took to be the best. The U.S. Figure Skating Association gave her a big boost by assigning her to the top international competition leading to the 1994 national championships. From the standpoint of an athlete training for the Olympics, Harding's pre-nationals season was almost perfect. The U.S. Figure Skating Association had picked her to participate in a week-long training camp in September 1993 at the Olympic ice rink in Hamar, Norway. The next month, she would travel to Dallas for Skate America International, which brought together all the Olympic favorites except for Nancy Kerrigan. Harding would skate in the NHK Trophy, a somewhat less high-powered event, scheduled to take place in December in Japan, that would be a perfect stage on which to fine-tune her programs. If she used it right, Harding could head to Detroit for the 1994 National Championships in the best competitive shape of her life.

But that perfect season turned into disaster for Harding. Troubled by money and marriage problems off the ice, she also was jinxed at the rink. She had skipped her normal summer vacation to continue training with her coach, Diane Rawlinson, at the Clackamas mall. New asthma medication had made remarkable improvements in Harding's breathing ability, and she said that for the first time she had an idea of how people with normal breathing felt. She had new music and new routines. As was her habit, Harding turned to movie scores for musical inspiration. Her short program was to the light and romantic theme from Kenneth Branagh's acclaimed *Much Ado About Nothing*. The long program would be skated to the brooding, dramatic theme from Steven Spielberg's blockbuster *Jurassic Park*.

Rawlinson, for her part, was looking forward to the training camp in Norway. It wasn't a competition, but Harding could get used to the peculiarities of the Olympic venue so they would be familiar if she returned in February 1994. The figure skating association, which paid for the athletes' trip to Norway and for their ice time, had chosen a handful of skaters to participate. Some were likely to make the 1994 Olympic team. Others might make a team in the future, and the camp was both an incentive and a reward for hard work.

Rawlinson and Harding were scheduled to leave from the Portland airport the morning of September 11. They planned to meet at the airport, and Rawlinson was on the freeway when she got a call from Harding on her car phone. The skater said she had spent the night in acute pain in a hospital emergency room. Doctors diagnosed it as a flare-up of an ovarian cyst, Harding said. She couldn't go to Norway.

The coach's immediate concern was for Harding, but Rawlinson knew she also had to contact U.S. Figure Skating Association officials to let them know the skater would have to drop out. Officials were initially sympathetic—until they learned that Harding skated in an exhibition in Cleveland only eight days later. The association considered demanding proof of her illness through medical reports but then decided to accept Harding's excuse.

"Tonya has talent, and we want to help her

along," said Jerry Lace, the USFSA's executive director. "But she has to try to help herself."

Tonya later told reporters she had refused doctors' advice to have surgery, since it would cost her six weeks of training. Although warned that the cyst could "explode" if she was under too much stress, Harding said that she would survive on pain medication until after the Olympics.

Meanwhile, her fan club raised more than $1,000 for Harding to take to Norway and gave it to her before she was to leave. Harding would never pay it back.

Harding arrived in Dallas for the October Skate America competition and immediately barged into controversy. She had dropped "Gillooly" as her last name, but she told reporters that, despite a divorce, "I am married." She also acknowledged smoking tobacco during the previous summer. "It was a stupid thing," she said. "I have stress. I'm a normal person like everyone else." But she drew the ire of skating association officials—and piqued the curiosity of reporters—when she claimed that the lack of financial support might destroy her Olympic campaign.

The skater said she had received only $10,000—from an anonymous donor—for her training that year. Harding made it clear that she blamed the U.S. Figure Skating Association for not supporting her. Unless she got more help, she might have to quit, Harding threatened.

In a corner of the press room, Kristin Matta listened incredulously. The USFSA's director of communication knew Harding's claims couldn't be true. She began digging though financial records and in a short time was able to tell reporters that Harding had received close to $40,000 in grants, prize money, and athlete subsistence over the past eleven months. And the skater had passed up a chance to skate the previous spring in a pro-am competition that paid a $20,000 appearance fee.

Harding backpedaled only slightly. She figured her financial year from March to March—the month of the world championships—she told reporters, and that meant she had received only $10,000.

The off-ice controversies might have kept hounding Harding if it weren't for her brilliant performance in the technical program of

Skate America. She was supposed to be only a second-string performer to the big show: a pre-Olympic look at reigning 1993 world gold medalist Oksana Baiul of Ukraine and France's Surya Bonaly, the world silver medalist. Skate America was Baiul's first big competition since the fifteen-year-old orphan with the expressive body and show-stopping style had burst on the scene in Prague. Bonaly, often dismissed as a purely athletic skater, had meanwhile matured in her style and for the first time was considered an Olympic contender.

Baiul was shaky in her short program, but she still had a slight lead over Bonaly. Then Harding skated onto the ice, her hair in a French braid and her brilliant orange costume radiating against the white of the ice. The Dallas Reunion Arena crowd had an American they could cheer for, and they applauded even before Harding's music began. When she finished two-and-a-half minutes later, the crowd went wild. The judges were equally enthusiastic. Heading into the long program, Skate America was Harding's to win.

Tonya was ecstatic after the program. It was the best she had skated, ever. She had proved those faceless doubters wrong again.

"I felt like I had to go out and prove I'm the Tonya Harding that people believed in and make sure they believe in me," Harding said after her triumph. "And I think they believe in me now. I think there were a few people out there who thought I was a has-been, because I haven't done anything win-wise in a few years."

The next night, Harding confidently skated onto the ice. With two triple jumps success-fully completed, she was almost halfway through her long program when she faltered just slightly. Briefly, she rocked her right skate side to side. Harding skated on, nailing a triple loop jump, then paused again—this time obviously having trouble with her skate. With less than a minute to go in her program, Harding skated over to the judges' table and, in the sudden silence of Reunion Arena, propped her right foot in front of head referee Sally-Anne Stapleford. The skate blade was loose, Harding complained. She couldn't skate on it.

Stapleford told Harding she could fix the blade and either start her program over again when all the other skaters had finished or pick up where she had left off. Harding chose the latter and skated to an entry gate, where she used a screwdriver to tighten the blade. Rawlinson saw the blade wobble, and she blamed the problem on putting new blades on a pair of old boots.

"When she came over to the side, it was so loose, if she'd gone on she would have hurt herself," Rawlinson said.

Harding said later that she didn't regret the decision to return immediately to skate, but she was distracted and had lost the important flow of the program. She fell on a double axel, turned a triple salchow into a double and, as she took her bows, cried.

Baiul crashed in her long program and still won the competition. Bonaly was second. Harding, so confident only minutes before, fell to third.

Harding returned to Portland, her money problems right beside her. Safeway Northwest Central Credit Union filed a claim against Harding and Gillooly for $1,984 owed to their Visa account, and in early November the credit union won a default judgment.

Meanwhile, the skater didn't have long before her next competition, the Northwest Pacific Regional Championships the first week of November, to be held on Harding's home ice at the Clackamas Town Center. A skater of Harding's caliber normally would have graduated from such low-level competitions years earlier, but her fourth-place finish at the 1993 national championships in March meant that she had to qualify to go to Detroit.

Publicly, Harding said she was excited to skate competitively in front of a hometown crowd. Promotions for the tournament were built around Harding competing and skating in a later exhibition. Young skaters who were used to skating in front of empty railings were thrilled at the prospect of the crowds Harding would attract. And Harding was practically guaranteed a victory since her rivals in the senior women's division had nowhere near her experience and skills. Her fan club worked with organizers so that a portion from each program sold went to Harding for training expenses. The printed programs included an autographed color picture of the skater. But in private, Harding was infuriated that she was required to skate in an event she considered beneath her. She repeatedly asked local skating officials to let her bypass the competition. One high-ranking skating official said she had to tell Harding several times that she was required to skate if she wanted to go to nationals. Harding had no choice. She couldn't get out of it.

Harding and the other senior women were preparing to warm up for the November 4 competition when a tournament referee called them over to the judges' table and told them the time of their event had been changed. Spectators were told that the women's competition had been moved from the afternoon to 9:30 p.m. that night, after the mall was closed. No explanation was given, but skaters and parents inside the rink immediately said the abrupt change had something to do with Tonya.

Their suspicions grew when rumors began to circulate among them that someone had telephoned a death threat, reportedly declaring that "If Harding skates, she'll get a bullet in the back." A handful of reporters, at the event to watch Harding, surrounded tournament official Joseph Driano for an explanation. What about the death threat against Tonya, one asked. Driano angrily refused to comment.

Harding quickly put on her street shoes and was escorted from the mall. But she returned in the early evening and met with her coaches, tournament officials, and mall security officers for almost an hour. When the meeting was over, and Harding had been whisked out of the mall again, Driano announced that indeed a death threat had been received against Harding and as a result she had been given a bye from the competition. The rest of the skaters would perform as planned.

Some officials at the rink were suspicious of the call almost immediately. That included Morry Stillwell, the USFSA second vice president who was overseeing the event.

"The circumstances were extremely strange," Stillwell said later. "We never knew, quite honestly."

What bothered Stillwell was that reporters knew the delay was because of a death threat to Harding, even though only a handful of people had been told about the call and officials hadn't given the information to anyone else at the rink.

"None of us said a word," Stillwell said. "None of us said anything about why we'd rescheduled it. It wasn't like 'Was it a death threat?' It was like, 'What about the death threat?' "

The next day, Harding issued a written statement, apologizing to her fans for having to cancel her appearance in the competition and a planned exhibition.

Harding was distraught over the incident, Rawlinson said. "She feels like this is her rink, this is her home," the coach said. "She feels really deflated now. She felt like this was a party on her own rink, and she was the hostess."

Soon after the competition, Morry Stillwell sent a letter to a few other USFSA members over a computer network. Friends of Harding saw the letter and gave her a copy. In the letter, Stillwell expressed his belief that the death threat had been staged. He noted that Harding was at the mall two days later, signing autographs. Not the kind of behavior you'd expect from someone who just had her life threatened, he wrote.

Harding's supporters blew up. Gillooly sent an angry response to Claire Ferguson, president of the USFSA. "The factual errors. . . . combined with his thinly veiled contention that Tonya or persons close to her authored the death threat—clearly indicate a lack of professionalism, objectivity, impartiality and intelligence on Mr. Stillwell's part," Gillooly wrote. "Mr. Stillwell's defamatory and inaccurate letter is despicable!"

Stillwell didn't change his mind. Soon after the death threat, Harding would hire Shawn Eckardt as her bodyguard.

Harding had still to qualify for the 1994 nationals. She was given the choice of competing at the Pacific Coast Sectional Championships or skating in the NHK Trophy in Japan, where she wouldn't have to finish in any particular place. Harding chose the tournament in Japan.

Twice-bitten in competitions that fall, Harding saw the NHK Trophy as only a final preparation for the nationals. She wasn't concerned about the competition—she and her coaches already had decided they wouldn't need the triple axel in Japan.

"It's something that, if it's solid like a rock, there's no reason for her not to do it," said coach Erika Bakacs, who would accompany Harding to Chiba, Japan. "She wants to do it. She's strong enough to do it."

Harding was relaxed and in good spirits. She joked about having to carry her own food to Japan because she was allergic to seafood. She did not feel pressure to win. She would do her best, she said. "It's important for me to see what I can do. It's not how I do, winning-wise; it's how I do for myself."

But disappointment struck again in Japan. Harding skated a clean short program but was left in seventh place. At least two skaters, Bonaly of France and China's Chen Lu, fell during their programs but were marked in third and fourth places, respectively. Three of the judges were in their first women's competition, Harding claimed. They didn't know what they were seeing.

"Both Erika and I felt like I was gypped," Harding said. "The rest fell on their butts."

Harding was terribly upset when she called Gillooly after the short program. She had skated well—better than the other skaters—and the judges had marked her down. They wouldn't let her win, even when she deserved it. Even though she managed to climb three places to fourth after the long program—a huge leap in an international competition—Harding brought her anger with her back to Portland.

Gillooly also was upset. While Tonya was still in Japan, he told his old friend Shawn Eckardt about the politics of elite figure skating, how everything depended on whether the right people liked you. Take Tonya, for instance, Gillooly said. She isn't the favorite at the national championships. Skating officials had assigned Harding and Nancy Kerrigan to different competitions because they were afraid Tonya would show up the East Coast Ice Queen, Gillooly said. They had even put Kerrigan on the cover of the USFSA magazine describing the national championships—as if she were guaranteed the U.S. and Olympic golds. She was going to win the national championship, no matter what, he said. That's what the leadership in figure skating had decided.

Eckardt listened to his friend and then wondered out loud: What if Nancy received some kind of threat?

7

A Plot Is Hatched

Shawn Eckardt loved the world of espionage. Sitting in his bedroom at his parents' house in a middle-class Portland neighborhood, he read the books he bought from special mail-order houses, books that described the operations of terrorists and how to silence an enemy. He told people he was in the personal safety business. His resume included counterterrorist work and international jobs protecting celebrities and potentates. He said he had been in the business for a decade.

It was all talk. Eckardt grew up in Portland, an undistinguished student through high school and at a nearby community college. Later, he would enroll at Executive Security Institute in Aspen, Colorado, where his classmates would make fun of his bragging and he was kicked out for lack of progress.

"He's a wannabe who wants to be king of

the mountain so bad he can taste it," said one veteran of Portland's personal protection industry. "He tried to impress me at every moment. He was always talking about the things he had done, the places he had gone and the money he had made. He claimed he had all this fancy computer equipment and could get information on anyone. He supposedly had the best photo equipment money could buy and had worked for foreign governments and had been in international counterespionage. And he said all this with a straight face. If you did the things he did, you wouldn't tell. You know my theory: The guy talks a good game and that's it."

When his friend Jeff Gillooly complained about the unfair treatment Tonya Harding had received at the hands of the international skating community, Eckardt drew on a fantasy world that was real to him. Threaten her rival, he said. Gillooly was receptive. He knew his wife had been upset when she was the victim of a death threat earlier that fall. Kerrigan too would fall apart, he reasoned.

Eckardt didn't want to let Harding in on the plan because he was afraid she would talk. But Gillooly said Harding, who was still in Japan at the NKH Trophy competition, would have to know. Otherwise, she could be psychologically affected when something happened to Kerrigan.

When Harding returned, the couple discussed Harding's having been snubbed by the U.S. Figure Skating Association when it needed another skater to fill out a pro-am competition. Skating in the event would have meant an appearance fee and, if she had placed well, thousands of dollars. Another, less experienced skater was chosen. Gillooly would later tell federal investigators that that was when he told Harding about his talk with Eckardt. They would benefit if Kerrigan couldn't skate, Gillooly remembered saying. Harding, he told FBI agents, agreed.

Gillooly was anxious to carry out the plan. He was mesmerized by the eventual windfall to Harding's career if her way was cleared to make the Olympic team and, eventually, to win a gold medal. Eckardt, for his part, saw a chance to generate business for his fledgling bodyguard company. Scared skaters would need bodyguards, he figured.

Just before Christmas, the two men talked on the telephone. Eckardt mentioned physical violence for the first time, that "taking her out" would be the solution. The best way, he said, would be to slice Kerrigan's Achilles' tendon. They would have to work quickly, though. The attack had to be done before Kerrigan left for the national championships, less than two weeks away. Gillooly wasn't sure he could pay for such a hit. He knew that George Steinbrenner, the owner of the New York Yankees and a patron of amateur athletes, had recently decided to take Harding under his wing. Gillooly had expected Steinbrenner to give Tonya almost $15,000 but was disappointed when he contributed only $10,000 through the U.S. Figure Skating Association. That wouldn't be enough to pay someone to hurt Kerrigan, Gillooly thought.

Eckardt came up with a cost estimate that included airplane and bus tickets, a car to use in Boston where the hit would take place, a hotel room, and food. It came to $4,500. Too much, Gillooly said. He could only afford a couple thousand dollars—unless he could persuade Steinbrenner to send more money for Harding. Until then, Gillooly wouldn't give the go-ahead.

Eckardt, meanwhile, set about assembling his "team"—without Gillooly's knowledge.

* * *

Derrick Brian Smith had lived most of his twenty-nine years in Portland, but in the fall of 1993 he had moved his wife Suzanne and her two sons to Phoenix, where he was a group home coordinator for Developmental Systems. In less than two months, Smith grew unhappy on his job. Ten days before Christmas, he quit.

Smith, balding, six-foot-one and two hundred fifty-eight pounds, had met Eckardt in the early 1980s, when both were students at Mount Hood Community College. The two became friends, although the relationship was strained for several years because Eckardt hadn't repaid $2,000 he owed to Smith. Derrick eventually wrote off the loss and renewed his friendship with Eckardt in 1988. The two shared a love for the world of spies, espionage and survivalism. They even talked about starting a survivalist school, where Eckardt could teach bodyguard work.

Smith was immediately interested when Eckardt called before Christmas to say he might have some bodyguard work, and maybe a job roughing up someone. Eckardt said he knew figure skater Tonya Harding. The skater's husband wanted bodyguards for

Harding at the national championships and afterward as she prepared for the Olympic Games. Money wasn't an object, Eckardt bragged. After all, George Steinbrenner was paying Harding's bills and Smith could count on $1,000 a week through the Olympics if Harding made the team.

Derrick Smith was all for it and ready to go. When Eckardt didn't call back in two days as he had said he would, Derrick called Eckardt's parents' home. Shawn's mother, Agnes, told Smith that her son had hurt his back and was in the hospital. Smith decided to seize the initiative. He called Jeff Gillooly and left a short message on his answering machine. Almost immediately, an alarmed Gillooly was on the telephone to Smith, who tried to explain that Eckardt was in the hospital and that now he, Smith, would take over the bodyguard team. Forget it, Gillooly said. He didn't know Smith. He only worked with Eckardt.

Two days before Christmas, Smith called his nephew, Shane Minoaka Stant, a hulking, two hundred forty-pound weight lifter who, like Smith, grew up in Oregon but had since moved to Phoenix. Smith had a job offer. When they had lived in the rural community of Corbett, east of Portland, Smith and the twenty-two-year-old Stant were known by their neighbors as survivalists who liked to dress in camouflage gear and "play army." One neighbor described Stant as "a big dude," with scars on his head from beatings as a child. Smith, the neighbor said, "is just different. He's not very sociable. He'd just walk by you and not say anything." Stant, who dabbled in martial arts, was arrested in October 1991 for taking a vehicle from an auto dealership in Coeur d'Alene, Idaho, and served fifteen days in a county jail. His uncle Derrick didn't have a criminal record.

Derrick explained that his employer wanted someone "taken down," not killed but hurt. Stant wanted more information; eventually Smith told him the job was to "take down a skater." Give me more details, Stant insisted. Ninety minutes later, Shawn Eckardt called Stant. Shane wanted specific information before he agreed to the hit. Eckardt told the weight lifter that he was to cut the Achilles' tendon of a figure skater. Forget it, Stant replied. He wouldn't cut anyone. But for the $2,500 Eckardt offered, he would hurt someone badly enough so she couldn't skate at the championships. Eckardt also offered the lure of a bodyguard contract worth $36,000. If his expenses were paid, he was on the job, Stant said.

On December 27, Smith and Stant drove to Portland in Derrick's black 1983 Porsche and checked into a cheap motel near Eckardt's parents' house. Eckardt called Gillooly to tell him that they should meet the next day, and he asked Jeff to bring specific information about Kerrigan, including a picture of the skater.

Tonya Harding wanted the attack on Kerrigan to happen at Nancy's home or skating rink, Gillooly would later tell the FBI. He ruled out Kerrigan's home—they couldn't call to find out the address without raising suspicion. Harding, he said, made up an excuse that she wanted information about Kerrigan's practice times so Kerrigan could sign a poster for a fan of Harding's. Then she telephoned a freelance writer from Pennsylvania named Vera Marano and asked if Marano could get her the address of Kerrigan's rink and when she practiced, Gillooly later said. Marano left a message on the couple's answering machine, but Harding and Gillooly thought it sounded like "Tunee Can Arena." Harding called Marano back and asked her to spell the name, and Gillooly said he watched as Harding wrote out "Tony Kent Arena."

Tonya drove the couple's big-wheel pickup and dropped Gillooly off at Eckardt's parents' house after her practice the next day, December 28. Before Gillooly's arrival, Eckardt had set up a tape recorder and covered it with a napkin. Smith wanted the tape for leverage if Gillooly decided not to pay.

After introductions, Gillooly told the others that Harding stood to make millions of dollars in endorsements if she won an Olympic gold medal. Gillooly wanted to make sure Harding made the team. To do that, he wanted Nancy Kerrigan knocked out of the national championships. Eckardt again talked of cutting Kerrigan's Achilles' tendon, but the others were against such a drastic act. Derrick Smith suggested hurting Kerrigan's arm, but Gillooly said to do it right, they had to hurt the skater's right leg—the one she depended on to take off and land her jumps. Without her jumps, she couldn't compete.

"Wouldn't it be easier just to kill her?" Eckardt asked, according to Gillooly's later account to authorities. Eckardt claimed he could set up a sniper who could do the job and vanish. Gillooly told Shawn to leave murder out of it. Talk about killing made him uncomfortable, Gillooly said.

Gillooly said he would pay $6,500, one third up front. There also was the promise of high-paying bodyguard work afterward, when Harding made the team. Eckardt guaranteed the hit, telling Gillooly he'd get his money back if it wasn't carried out before the championships. At the end of the meeting, Smith and Stant shook Gillooly's hand. "It was a pleasure," Stant said. They were the only words he uttered during the meeting.

Smith and Stant talked about the plot as they returned to their hotel. They felt bad that Kerrigan would be hurt—she'd done nothing to deserve it. But, they reasoned, if they didn't do the job, Eckardt and Gillooly would find someone else to do it, someone who would have no inhibitions about seriously hurting the skater. They would do the job, they agreed, but they'd make sure Kerrigan wasn't hurt too badly. She'd be okay.

Harding was waiting in their truck as Gillooly prepared to leave. Eckardt hugged him, saying, "We're going to make a lot of money. We're going to make a lot of money."

As they drove away, Tonya asked how the

meeting went, Jeff later told the FBI. When he told her about Eckardt's money-back guarantee, Harding laughed. This, Gillooly said, was better than playing the lottery. Gillooly remembered that they were driving past a public storage building when he said, "I think we should go for it."

"Okay, let's do it," he recalled Harding replying.

When they arrived home, Gillooly said Harding called the Tony Kent Arena and first got a prerecorded message. She tried a second number and talked to a woman who told her Kerrigan's normal practice times. A manager at the Tony Kent Arena later said people called regularly with questions about Kerrigan and there was no way to know if Harding, or anyone else, had called on a certain day.

The next evening, Gillooly and Harding drove to Eckardt's house with pictures of Nancy Kerrigan and the information about her practice times. While Harding talked to Eckardt's mother, Shawn told Gillooly that the plan already was in action. Two men—not the same ones Gillooly had met, Eckardt assured him—would carry out the hit. One was prepared to fly out of Seattle to Boston that night. The other would fly out of Los

Angeles. Gillooly took $2,000 he had withdrawn earlier from his bank and laid the money, in hundred dollar bills, on Eckardt's desk.

In reality, it was Stant who later left Portland on an American Airlines jet that took him to Dallas and then to Boston. He carried a packet with background information on Kerrigan and a "glamour" photograph of the skater. Upon arrival, Stant checked into a hotel near Logan International Airport, using a credit card and registering under his own name. He discovered that the credit card he shared with his girlfriend couldn't be used to rent a car, and so he had to wait a day for his own card to arrive from Phoenix.

On December 31, the next day, Stant found the Tony Kent Arena in the resort town of South Dennis on Cape Cod. For two days, he parked outside the arena, moving his car every thirty minutes but always keeping an eye on the front door. On January 3, Stant called the rink and asked about Nancy Kerrigan, and whether she would be skating soon. He claimed to have a daughter who wanted to see Kerrigan skate. The woman told him Kerrigan had left for the national championships.

Stant drove back to Boston, returned his

rental car, and took a cab to the train station—
where he learned that no trains were going to
Detroit. His money getting low, he took a cab
to the Greyhound Bus Station and bought a
$125 ticket to Detroit. The twenty-five-hour
trip would bring him to Detroit late January 4.

Stant checked into a Super 8 Motel, registering in his own name and paying $101.76
for three nights. He asked for a waterbed and
paid $10.39 for a video player and two adult
movies, *Hollywood Fantasies* and *The Girls
of Beverly Hills*. Once in his room, Stant
called Smith, who had in the meantime
returned to Phoenix.

Back in Portland, Tonya Harding and Jeff
Gillooly were beginning to suspect that the
would-be hit men had taken their money and
run, Gillooly later said. As late as December
30, Harding said it would be nice if they
could "get" Kerrigan in a bar on New Year's
Eve, so Kerrigan would "look bad" to the
public, Gillooly recalled. But on New Year's
Day, during a late night private practice session at Clackamas Town Center, Gillooly
said, Harding skated up to the railing where
he and Eckardt stood talking. Why wasn't the

job getting done? she demanded of Eckardt. "If it doesn't get done, you call them and get the $2,000 back," Gillooly recalled Harding as having said.

Eckardt made up stories to keep the couple pacified. The hit men had broken into Kerrigan's car to get her address off her registration while she was at a 7-Eleven and, when the skater came out the door, stole the car. Later, Eckardt claimed, the men hid in Kerrigan's house on New Year's Eve, but she didn't come home. Gillooly told Eckardt to tell the men they would receive a $10,000 bonus if the job was done in a hurry, and he showed a $10,000 check from the U.S. Figure Skating Association—money that was donated by Steinbrenner.

On January 3, the day Stant left Boston, an angry Gillooly called Eckardt demanding to know what was happening. Eckardt said he had talked to Derrick Smith and the "two guys" had gone to the skating rink but Kerrigan wasn't there. They were told that Kerrigan was taking quiet time before nationals, Eckardt said. When Harding heard this tale, she blew up, Gillooly later said. Harding, according to Gillooly, had then called the Tony Kent Arena and learned that Kerrigan had skated early that morning; Harding was convinced she and Gillooly had lost their $2,000, Gillooly would later tell authorities.

Gillooly called Eckardt, demanding the money back. He didn't believe that anyone was even in Boston. Eckhardt sought to calm his friend. The attack would be done; it would happen at the national championships.

Gillooly arrived home late the night of January 4 to find a message on his answering machine. "Jeff, this is Shane. We met in Shawn's office about a week ago. I'm in Detroit. Call me at this number." Gillooly hit the roof and called Eckardt. You told me he was not one of the people sent to get Kerrigan, Gillooly told his friend. Eckardt claimed Gillooly was mistaken. It was "Lance," Shane's older brother and "the more violent of the two," who was in Detroit. Eckardt thought that since Gillooly didn't believe anyone was in Boston, "Lance" should call.

The job couldn't be done in Detroit, Gillooly insisted. There was too much security at the championships. It would be impossible to get close enough to the skaters—let alone get away after attacking one. "Lance" didn't have enough money to go home, Eckardt said. He would finish the job so Gillooly would pay the rest of the money, then leave.

Gillooly offered to pay the man's trip home, but later the two wired about $725 of Gillooly's money to Smith in Phoenix.

The next day, Smith flew to Detroit and met Stant at the Joe Louis Arena. The two went into the nearby Cobo Ice Arena, where skaters practiced. Stant watched where the skaters left the rink, then walked down to the supposedly secured area. For forty-five minutes, Stant wandered around an area that was off-limits without being stopped. He took note of a hallway leading to a set of open, Plexiglas doors.

Smith and Stant then drove to the Westin Hotel at the Renaissance Center, where Kerrigan, Harding, and the other skaters in the championships stayed. A readerboard said a skaters' meeting was being held on the fifth floor, and Stant took the elevator up but found only an empty room. Back at the Super 8 Motel, Smith called Eckardt and learned that Harding had seen a man in the hotel lobby whose appearance had frightened her. Her description of the man matched that of Stant.

It wouldn't do to have Tonya upset; it was Nancy Kerrigan, after all, whom they sought to hurt.

Tom Treick

FLYING HIGH: *Harding's career seemed ready to take off in 1985, when at 14 she already was competing in the featured seniors competition.*

Tom Treick

MOVING UP: *Competing in her second national championship in 1987 (above), Harding finished fifth in Tacoma. In 1990 (right), she was second after compulsories, but hampered by pneumonia in the free skate, finishing seventh overall.*

Tom Treick

TRIPLE CROWN:
At the top of her sport, Harding is all smiles (left) after landing her historic triple axel en route to the 1991 national championship. Below, Harding is flanked by runner-up Kristi Yamaguchi and Nancy Kerrigan, who finished third.

Tom Treick

Tom Treick

NO MEDAL: *Harding and her coach, Dody Teachman, were disappointed with her fourth-place finish in the 1992 Winter Olympics.*

Tom Treick

Tom Treick (2)

HARD TIMES: *Problems stalked Harding in 1993. First, she fell in a performance in Phoenix (above), then a problem with a loose skate blade cost her a chance to win Skate America in Dallas (right).*

Doug Beghtel

Doug Beghtel

BACK ON TOP: *For the moment at least, all is right in Harding's world as she celebrates winning the 1994 national championship in Detroit.*

BEST-LAID PLANS:
Harding returns from the nationals, accompanied by sometime bodyguard Shawn Eckardt, who later implicated both Harding and ex-husband Jeff Gillooly in the plot to injure Nancy Kerrigan.

Brent Wojahn

ECKARDT VISIT:
Harding and Gillooly leave Eckardt's house the day after Harding arrived back from competition in Detroit.

Brent Wojahn

Tom Treick

LENDING AN EAR: *Diane Rawlinson, who began working with Harding when the skater was 3 1/2, offers some advice.*

THE PLAYERS: *1st row (left to right): Jeff Gillooly; Shawn Eckardt; Derrick Smith; Shane Stant; 2nd row (left to right): Robert Weaver; Ronald Hoevet; Nancy Kerrigan*

Steve Nehl

FUTURE TENSE: *Even with Rawlinson's guidance, Harding's career has unquestionably been hurt by the investigation into the attack on Kerrigan.*

8

Triumph Without Victory

Tonya Harding knew the 1994 figure skating championships would be her last chance to grab a piece of the success that Kristi Yamaguchi and Nancy Kerrigan had already found. After two decades of skating as an amateur, Harding planned to turn pro after the season. She looked forward to teaching and touring in ice shows but was under pressure to come up with those last big victories. She felt she had to win—she corrected people when they told her she could finish No. 2 and still make the Olympic team—and her training sessions at the mall reflected her determination.

For most of her adult career, Harding seemed to spend more time talking to coaches on the sidelines than actually skating. Typically, Harding would warm up with a spin, talk to Rawlinson, try a jump, talk to Rawlinson, and so on for an hour or ninety minutes.

Some spectators wondered how Harding could improve with such disjointed sessions, but the stop-and-go practice was common with other experienced skaters, as well. They had done their programs so many times, they didn't need to practice the whole routine. Instead, they worked on particular jumps or moves that were rough or difficult and let it all come together in competition.

Harding, however, had been caught in the 1992 Olympics with too little preparation. She and her coaches said it was different now. Tonya worked hard and, as fall turned into winter, began doing complete run-throughs of her programs during practice. Even though the skater continued to smoke, her asthma was under control and the run-throughs helped build her endurance. Without fail, she ended each session with a string of triple axel jumps.

Her coaches were proud of her, Tonya told friends. Financially, things were looking up, too. Dorothy Baker, a member of the Delaware Olympic Committee, had heard about Harding's money woes that fall and the death threat at the Northwest regionals. Baker talked to George Steinbrenner, owner of the New York Yankees and a USOC vice president who had sponsored athletes in the past. Steinbrenner gave about $20,000 to Harding to help with her training. A Portland donor also gave her $10,000, and promoter Tom Collins sent her an additional $10,000.

For Christmas, Harding and Jeff Gillooly decorated a small tree with colored balls and laughed when they discovered their black cat, Ace, hiding in the branches. Harding bought Gillooly a Nintendo game, and he spent hours working the controls in a video contest between the Portland Trail Blazers and the Chicago Bulls. Gillooly bought jewelry for Harding.

Her practice routines weren't the only things different about Harding in the days leading up to the Detroit competition. Like athletes in every sport, Harding always had a pat, self-effacing answer when questioned about her goals for an upcoming competition. She would do her best, Harding said, and be happy with that.

The new Harding talked a bigger talk. She would win the national title. Then she would win the Olympic gold. After that, she would get what was due to her—the paycheck for twenty years of hard work. She chided a reporter: "There's no 'hopefully.' I'm going.

Nobody's going to stop me."

Days before she was to leave for Detroit, Harding sat at her dining-room table, talking about the Olympic Games and the upcoming championships. Fog shrouded the steep valley outside the modest cabin tucked among cedar and fir trees almost a mile off a country road. Neighbors were out of hollering distance, and, on this winter afternoon, their homes weren't even visible. The cabin gave Harding what she craved, quiet and solitude.

The living room, dining area and kitchen of the cabin were open. Two pictures of Jeff and Tonya, one from their wedding, were displayed prominently. In both pictures they were holding each other.

Less visible were the signs of Harding's skating career. Only when you looked close did you see the winner's crystal bowl from the 1991 U.S. championships, which now held sewing materials and other knick-knacks. A blue piggy bank, from the 1993 championships, stood on a counter.

The skater liked the circumstance that she was headed to Detroit as the underdog. "I'm just tired of people saying, 'She can't do it,'" Harding said. "I like the pressure. I'm the underdog again, and I like that. I get to walk out with a gold medal for nationals and a gold medal for the Olympics."

For once, Harding was one of the less interesting stories as skaters gathered in Detroit. Nancy Kerrigan was in the best shape of her life as she prepared to defend her title. Elaine Zayak, a twenty-eight-year-old with a Valley Girl voice and bobbing ponytail, delighted reporters as she attempted an amateur comeback more than a decade after winning the 1982 World Championship. At the other end of the age spectrum, thirteen-year-old Michelle Kwan brought more than just promise to her second senior nationals.

Everyone knew Detroit would be Nancy Kerrigan's show.

The elegant, beautiful Kerrigan already was the American Olympic hopeful when she tumbled badly during the 1993 World Championship, finishing a crushing fifth in Prague. When she came off the ice after skating a ninth-place performance in her long program, a distraught Kerrigan asked her coach if she could skate it again. Because of Kerrigan's poor performance, the United States would send only two women to the Olympic Games instead of the three it had sent to the last four Winter Games. Kerrigan already had an

Olympic medal, the bronze she had won in 1992. She was—or would become—a wealthy woman, with endorsement contracts with Campbell's Soup, Seiko, Reebok and Evian. She had her gap-toothed smile fixed with caps.

Many saw Kerrigan's classic looks—the high cheekbones that made her look more like Katharine Hepburn with every passing year— and assumed the skater was from blueblood stock. But her upbringing was strictly blue collar. Her father, Dan, had had to take on extra jobs to pay for his daughter's skating. Her mother, Brenda, was legally blind. Kerrigan learned to skate at a nearby community rink and often joined her brothers in hockey games. The family took out a second mortgage on their home so Kerrigan could pursue her dream.

Kerrigan and Harding's upbringing might have been similar, but Nancy had something Tonya searched in vain for: family support. The Kerrigan family always was close; her parents always were around to help pick Nancy up and comfort her. Kerrigan and Harding rose at the same time in national-level skating. Harding was the better skater, most with knowledge of the sport agreed, but her inconsistency showed in head-to-head competitions, where Kerrigan held a 7-2 edge. In 1993, with Kristi Yamaguchi skating for money in professional shows, the shy Kerrigan, uncomfortable with the newfound attention, ascended the nation's ice throne.

After the debacle in Prague, Kerrigan returned to her Cape Cod home determined to overcome doubts about her mental and skating strength. She began seeing a sports psychologist, who helped the skater build self-confidence and concentration. On the ice, Kerrigan worked on her jumps. She would prove that she wasn't just a pretty skater, as some detractors said.

Only a season ago, Kerrigan did runthroughs of her programs, always leaving something out—a jump, a spin, or footwork. It wasn't because she couldn't do it. She was afraid—of failing. In the weeks before Detroit, Kerrigan did perfect, complete runthroughs. Once she even had her coach rewind the music so she could do her long program three times in a row. She nailed seventeen of eighteen triple jumps.

Kerrigan wasn't afraid anymore.

"She's never worked this hard in her life," her coach said. "When she skates, I really see someone who needs a bigger ice rink—and that's the essence of ice skating." Kerrigan told reporters she expected to win. "I've trained really hard for this and I've worked for a long time."

Someone asked her to compare her style to Harding's. "I'm glad I'm not a judge," Kerrigan said. "They all have their own opinions. It's not like we're running against a clock. You'd have to ask the judges."

A sprinkling of snow had turned into a blizzard that first week of January 1994 in Detroit.

About two hundred people, including groups of children from Detroit-area schools, sat bundled against the cold in the Cobo Ice Arena to watch the championship women practice. Practices were free, and for many fans it was their only chance to see skaters up close. People wandered around the arena looking for good spots to take pictures or to get the autograph of a skater. Although there were skating officials and coaches around the rink, there were no security guards in sight.

Group B of the championship women was sheduled to begin its practice at 1 p.m.,

Thursday, January 6. Tonya Harding, looking relaxed and smiling, was among the group. One by one, the skaters' long program music was played so they could practice their routine. Harding was last, and she stood in place at center ice as the ominous opening notes of her music from Jurassic Park rumbled out of the loud speakers.

Harding started to skate her routine, then stopped and said loud enough for spectators to hear, "That's not my music." She skated over to the practice official and argued that the tape being played was not the right version of her music.

Normally, a piece is played through only once. Officials agreed to play a different tape of Harding's music, but her good mood was gone. Rawlinson later discovered the error—a music mixing company had sent in the wrong version of "Jurassic Park" without the coach's approval—and made sure officials had Harding's correct music. Harding left the rink to go to her hotel for a nap as Group C of the championship women, including Nancy Kerrigan, took the ice for their practice session.

The practice was uneventful. Kerrigan, wearing a white costume with lacy, long sleeves and with a white tie holding her hair back, skated through her long program while her parents watched.

Dana Scarton was waiting for Kerrigan to come off the ice. Scarton, a sports reporter for the *Pittsburgh Post-Gazette*, was going to cover her first Olympic Games in Lillehammer. She had never reported on figure skating before and was hoping to grab a quick interview with Kerrigan.

The U.S. Figure Skating Association normally is protective of its skaters during the championships. Reporters had to wear picture identification and were restricted to certain areas. Skaters were brought to a press room after a competition, or reporters could make requests for certain athletes through the association's media relations staff. But practices were more relaxed. Even though Scarton was in an area that was off-limits to reporters, no one questioned her presence.

Kerrigan was the last skater to leave the ice. She put plastic guards on her skate blades and stepped through a curtain where Scarton waited to introduce herself.

No one noticed the man in the black jacket and jeans stand up from his seat as Kerrigan walked below him with an ABC cameraman following her. When the cameraman set his camera on the floor, the man walked past him and then past two other men who were talking in the hallway.

Just as Scarton was about to ask a question, the burly man rushed from behind the women, crouching to club Kerrigan above her right knee. He swung the weapon with both hands like a baseball bat. People out in the arena heard the blow.

Then they heard Kerrigan's screams.

The man rushed past startled witnesses down a hallway to a set of locked doors and used his head as a battering ram to break through a Plexiglas window, escaping into the snowy city.

People immediately gathered around the sobbing Kerrigan. Dan Kerrigan lifted his daughter in his arms.

"It hurts, Dad," Kerrigan cried. "It hurts so bad."

Kerrigan was rushed to a hospital, where an initial examination showed that the blow had badly bruised, but did not seriously damage, the muscle just above her right knee. She was able to walk and went back to her hotel.

The fact that the attack was clearly aimed at Kerrigan's skating ability—she takes off from and lands her jumps on her right leg—wasn't lost on reporters, who gossiped that it looked like the work of a rival's fans. A *Sports Illustrated* writer joked, "Probably Tonya Harding's thugs." But Abby Haight of *The Oregonian* was more specifically worried. What did the attacker look like? she asked Scarton. When Scarton described the man as at least six feet tall and two hundred pounds, Haight was relieved. That ruled out Joe Haran, Harding's obsessed supporter.

Meredith Meyer was outside the Cobo Ice Arena when she heard the crash of the Plexiglas panel hitting the ground. "I heard these screams," Meyer later said. "Then someone was yelling, "Stop him! Stop him!' "

Meyer saw the man crawl through the door. He stood only a few feet from her, both hands gripping what she thought was a crowbar. She couldn't see his face, but he was frightening. Before Meyer could react, the man dashed in the direction of the Joe Louis Arena, near the Detroit River waterfront.

Meyer and other witnesses gave detectives the description of a powerfully built man, but their accounts varied wildly. Four said he was white; two said the thug was a light-skinned black. The police eventually issued two composite drawings of their suspect. When reporters saw them they laughed. One drawing looked like a square-jawed white man. One drawing looked like a delicate, oval-faced black woman.

The man with the club could be anyone.

Never mind, police indicated. Technology would come to the rescue. Through special "space age" techniques, video taken right after the attack would provide a clear picture of the assailant. Computers would enhance the tiny, blurred image of the man fleeing from the downed skater.

For days, the Detroit police talked about this miracle of science, but when it was finally done the result looked only vaguely human—reporters dubbed it "the shroud of Detroit." Police, however, declared that their suspect was conclusively white and had long hair. (The eventual confessed assailant fit neither of these specifics.)

The attack threw the championships into turmoil.

When it was clear Kerrigan wasn't seriously injured, the U.S. Figure Skating Association called a press conference with Kerrigan's agent, Jerry Solomon; Dr. Steven Plomaritis, who treated the skater; Atanas Ilitch, the vice president of Olympia Arenas, which operated the Cobo Ice Arena; and Cliff Russell, a representative of Detroit Mayor Dennis Archer.

The men answered questions about security—"Security was very high," Ilitch said, which led to the inevitable question: High on what?

Kerrigan's coach said he had run up and down a hall looking in vain for an officer after Kerrigan was hit, and reporters knew that identifying credentials were rarely checked.

Russell said Detroit police already were working feverishly to find the assailant. Plomaritis described the injury in physician's jargon, and when reporters complained that they couldn't understand him, Plomaritis used a reporter's knee to show where the blow fell.

But no one knew why the attack had occurred.

"She's never been threatened," Solomon said. "She gets a lot of letters that say a lot of things. There are a lot of crazy people saying crazy things out there, but there's never been anything that has fightened her or I."

For Kerrigan, the attack did more than damage her leg. She would probably not be able to skate in the championships and risked losing a sure spot on the Olympic team and her chance to prove herself to an international audience. USFSA rules allow a medical waiver for an athlete to join an Olympic squad, but only if the athlete had won a medal in the previous world championships. Claire Ferguson, president of the USFSA, said it looked as if Kerrigan would have to skate.

By Friday morning, skating was out of the question for Kerrigan. Physicians drained blood and fluid from her knee, but it still was swollen and tender. She could not count on the knee to hold her on a glide, let alone a jump.

"She was not able to bend the knee fully," said Dr. Mahlon Bradley, an orthopedic surgeon for the USFSA, who examined Kerrigan on Friday morning. "She certainly did not have strength in her knee. When we asked her to do a simple hop test, she couldn't even control that."

At the same time, Ferguson said Kerrigan could indeed be appointed to the Olympic team. Reporters scanning the association's rule book the night before had found a simple answer to Kerrigan's eligibility problems. The rule stated that the association's forty-five-member International Committee could appoint any skater it wanted to the Olympic team. The appointment couldn't be made until after the women's championship was completed, but for all intents and purposes, Kerrigan was Lillehammer-bound.

Ferguson said the young women preparing to skate that night in the technical portion of the championships knew they might be fighting for only one Olympic berth.

"I told them they had worked hard," Ferguson said. "They had earned their position. And even though this could be very hard, I wanted them to do their best."

By midday Friday, the skating association had issued 250 additional media credentials. When Kerrigan walked stiff-legged, but without a limp, to a table to answer reporter's questions, the press room was jammed.

No, she had no idea who could have carried out the brutal attack. Brenda Kerrigan earlier had mentioned that her daughter had received two letters from a fan in Ontario, Canada, across the river from Detroit. The first letter, sent after the Olympics, was smutty, Brenda Kerrigan said. The second was angry that the skater hadn't replied. Nancy Kerrigan didn't remember the letters as vividly as her mother. She had never been afraid of fans.

Kerrigan made a pitch to the International Committee. "I've worked so hard. I've never worked so hard as I did this year," she said. "I've won both competitions I've been in this year. I train really hard. I've never skated as well as I've been skating."

She wanted back on the ice. She wanted the chance to show people that Prague was just four bad minutes—not a career. Kerrigan was not afraid to skate. The attack had nothing to do with being on the ice, she said.

"I know I'm going to be okay," she said. "It's really hard to be less of a public person. Since this happened, I've been on the news every half-hour. If people didn't know who I was before, they do now.

"It's hard to say how long I'll look over my shoulder to see who's behind me."

Meanwhile, Tonya Harding had tried hard to put the attack out of her mind. It was always easy for her to focus on skating, to block out distractions except for the applause. Nancy Kerrigan and the still-unidentified attacker were distractions. As she glided to the center of the rink at Joe Louis Arena the next night, it was only Tonya and the ice.

She was in the same red costume she had worn at the 1993 national championships, the one that had embarrassingly come apart on a jump. Harding had designed it, as she did all her newer costumes. Her sister-in-law, Michelle Enyardt, did the sewing.

Figure skating is a sport of illusion, and wearing the same costume twice—especially at such a major event—broke an unwritten fashion rule. Harding looked gauche.

But she skated like the champion she intended to be. From the soaring triple lutz-double toe jump combination that opened her technical program to the dizzying spin that closed it, Harding looked confident. All nine judges ranked her first.

"I had a lot of speed and confidence," Harding said later. "Everything flowed right together. I have the experience, and maybe that gives me an edge. But nobody expected me to do anything here."

Nicole Bobek, a sixteen-year-old known for her unpredictable but crowd-pleasing skating, was second behind Harding. But with Kerrigan watching from a private skybox, Harding clearly owned the competition.

* * *

Tonya Harding had a new dress for the long program. Her coaches had not seen it; it was Harding's own design and she was excited. Figure skaters usually bring backup costumes to big competitions, but the notoriously stubborn Harding had brought just this one. Harding had to do things her way, even if it was the wrong way. The USFSA Rulebook stipulated, "Costumes must be modest, dignified and appropriate for athletic competition. Costumes, however, may reflect the character of the music chosen."

Diane Rawlinson cringed when she saw the outfit. The deep purple dress was sleeveless, trimmed with gold sequins. The flesh-colored net in the front not only plunged to Tonya's navel, it stretched from armpit to armpit. The illusion was not elegant; the curves of the underside of her breasts were clearly visible.

When Harding stepped onto the ice for her warm-up, one reporter quipped that the costume looked as if it belonged on a hooker. At least two judges marked Harding down for the trampy outfit, but it didn't matter. Tonya Harding was the U.S. champion.

Harding was the last on the ice. She knew it would take a major mistake to lose the gold, and she had no intention of risking that. There would be no triple axel. She would skate conservatively. "I was on automatic," she later recalled. "It was just, go out there and do the program the way I've trained for it."

Harding opened with a sweeping triple lutz jump. Skating to the other end of the rink, she planned to do a double axel. Instead, she turned the jump into a single axel, making a face as she landed on the ice. Instead of falling apart, Harding hit four more triple jumps and a double axel, lit up the center ice with her spins and then pumped her fist with the certainty that the title was hers.

Harding smiled and waved in the embrace of more than 17,000 cheering fans. She was back in control and back on top, as she had planned.

The skater started coughing as she waited in the kiss-and-cry area for the scores that would confirm what everyone in the arena knew. When ABC commentator Julie Moran put a microphone into Harding's face, the skater gasped out, "I proved I am the Tonya Harding who everyone always believes in. I know who my real friends are," before breaking into another coughing fit. Reporters watching the scene on a television in the pressroom wondered at the bizarre statement. Who were Tonya's real friends? Michelle Kwan finished second. As expected, Kerrigan was appointed to the Olympic team and Kwan, the U.S. hopeful for years to come, graciously deferred to Kerrigan. "What I got was incredible, already," the thirteen-year-old said.

Harding's hacking fit delayed the medal ceremony but, still coughing, the skater finally made it to her press conference with the gold medal around her neck.

It wasn't an asthma attack, Harding insisted. Suddenly stopping after such physical exertion had brought on the fit. Her answers to reporters were punctuated by coughing and gasping.

The victory wasn't complete, Harding acknowledged. "It won't be a complete title without being able to go against Nancy," she said.

But the night was complete in other ways. Jeff Gillooly had arrived at Harding's hotel late that afternoon and was able to watch his ex-wife skate and, later, join her celebration.

9

The Conspiracy Unravels

Shane Stant was a powerful enough man that he could do plenty of damage to a five-foot-four figure skater with his bare hands, but he had brought a weapon with him to Detroit. Called an Asp baton, it was a black wand that telescoped out with a whip-like motion of the hand. He had bought the lethal-looking weapon at a store called Spy Headquarters in Mesa, Arizona.

Stant awoke at 7 a.m. on January 6. He dressed in a dark brown shirt, black jeans, brown hiking boots, a black leather jacket, and a black baseball cap. He tucked the Asp into his pants and pulled on a pair of black leather gloves. He carried a note that Eckardt had put together, reading, "All skating whores will die. No one can shut me off." The note included the names of several elite skaters, including Nancy Kerrigan and Tonya Harding. Stant planned to drop the note after he hit

Kerrigan so that investigators would think the attack was the work of a deranged fan.

Derrick Smith drove Stant to the Cobo Ice Arena, where they plotted their escape plan for the first time. They pried the license plates off a car in a downtown Detroit parking garage and placed them over the license plates of their rental car. At the arena, Stant pointed out the doors he would leave through after the attack was accomplished. Smith parked near the doors and the two went into the Cobo Ice Arena. Stant sat near the skaters' entrance. Smith found a seat on the opposite side of the rink.

The pair knew when Kerrigan was practicing because Jeff Gillooly had told them after getting the times from Harding, Gillooly would later recount. They had considered doing the job in Kerrigan's hotel room—first attacking her and then leaving her tied up with duct tape—and Harding had gotten the room number from a clerk, Gillooly said. But it was too far from the hotel elevators to the exit doors. The practice rink would be safer.

Stant planned to signal Smith when Kerrigan took to the ice so that Derrick would know to get the car and have it ready. The pair watched as one group of skaters, including

Tonya, practiced. It wasn't until late in the session when the announcer gave her name and she began practicing her program that Smith figured out which skater was Tonya. After a short break, the second group of skaters were ready to practice. Shortly before 2 p.m., the announcer began reading the names of the skaters. When Kerrigan's name was announced, and Kerrigan stepped onto the ice, Stant stood up. It was the signal. Smith left the arena.

The skaters practiced for about forty-five minutes. Kerrigan was one of the last to leave the ice. She stopped at the entry gate to put on plastic blade protectors. An ABC cameraman, filming the practice as part of the network's coverage of the championships, followed her as she walked toward a blue curtain that led to the dressing areas. So did Stant. The cameraman set down his camera and Stant slipped behind him on the right. He walked past two men who were talking. Ahead, Kerrigan had stopped to talk to a reporter.

Stant took the baton in his right hand and the note in his left and walked quickly up to Kerrigan. The skater instinctively took a step back as the stranger approached, but Stant swung the baton, striking her about an inch above her right knee. Kerrigan immediately fell to the ground, screaming. The blow was glancing, however, and Stant hit with only about half the force he could have used. He told Smith later that he knew he hadn't hurt Kerrigan badly because he didn't hear the popping noise of a bone breaking.

Stant moved past the shrieking Kerrigan, dropping the note as he broke into a run toward the doors he had seen on his earlier survey of the hall. As he neared the doors, he saw that they were chained together. Panicked, Stant charged through the bottom of the door like a football tackle, popping the Plexiglas out of its frame and sending himself sprawling onto the sidewalk. From behind, he heard someone shout, "Somebody stop him."

Nearby, a large line of people waited for a bus. Stant scrambled off the pavement and began running, knocking down one man who tried to step in his way. As he ran, he threw the baton under a car, where its landing was muffled by five inches of freshly fallen snow.

Smith and Stant had agreed that Smith would wait a few blocks away at a post office. Stant would run to the post office after the attack. But Smith parked the car only about one hundred fifty yards from the doors Stant had planned to escape through. When he saw someone being pushed, he assumed Stant had made it out. Stant ran down the sidewalk toward the post office—and away from Smith who had to drive after Stant.

Stant looked back. No one had followed him.

After getting rid of the stolen license plates at a gas station, Smith and Stant headed back to their motel room. Gillooly and Eckardt already had made arrangements to wire $1,300 to Detroit, and late that night Smith took a cab to a Western Union office to pick it up. When he returned to the motel, Smith bought some beer and reserved tickets on a flight to Phoenix the next day. The pair had their alibi, if they needed it. They would tell anyone who asked that they had been hired to watch Harding. Her husband suspected her of infidelity, they would say.

The telephone woke Gillooly at about noon Thursday in Portland. It was Harding, calling from Detroit, Gillooly later told the FBI.

"It happened," Harding said.

"What happened?" a groggy Gillooly asked.

"Nancy. They did it," she replied.

Gillooly was surprised. "You're kidding."

Harding wasn't kidding. "Did they get away?" Gillooly asked.

Harding didn't know.

Tonya described the attack to Gillooly much as her coach, Diane Rawlinson, had told her. Rawlinson was still at the rink when the assault occurred and had talked to Frank Carroll, the coach of Michelle Kwan, who had been nearby. Some man had come out of nowhere and hit Nancy in the leg with a club, an upset Rawlinson told Harding.

Gillooly then broke the news to Eckardt over the telephone; afterward he withdrew $3,000 from his bank account and drove over to his friend's house. Gillooly was worried about how Smith and Stant would get out of Detroit. Eckardt said his mother, Agnes, had taken care of the flight arrangements. All they had to do was wire the men $1,300. Agnes Eckardt knew all the details of the plot, Gillooly later told the FBI.

On their way to wire the money, Eckardt spun a wild tale of the attack for Gillooly. Smith and Shane had beat up a journalist at a bar the night before and stolen his credential, Eckardt said. They took care of a security guard by wrapping him in duct tape. When

Nancy Kerrigan came through the door, Shane had burst from a crowd of about one hundred people and had hit her on the knee cap three times and on the side of her leg twice. When she fell to the ground, he had hit her in the head with what Eckardt called a Cobra baton. While he struck her, Shane had shouted, "I spent twenty-nine hours on a bus for you, bitch," Eckardt claimed. And when he ran out on the sidewalk, Stant had had to beat up one guy. Meanwhile, Derrick was standing nearby. He drew his gun and pretended to be an off-duty policeman, shouting, "Stop! Police!" as he chased Shane.

On Saturday, January 8, Gillooly flew to Detroit on a Delta Air Lines jet; he took a stack of Eckardt's business cards with him. He had promised Eckardt that he would pass them around; World Bodyguard Services Inc. was bound to get business.

Gillooly got to watch Harding skate a beautiful long program, winning the national title and assuring herself the coveted position on the Olympic team. Gillooly was standing in a hallway with Harding after the victory when they were approached by Detective Dennis

Richardson of the Detroit Police Department. Richardson was interested in talking to the couple when they had a few free moments Sunday.

That night, Gillooly caught a glimpse of Kerrigan. Suddenly, he felt very small, he would say later.

Gillooly met with Richardson at about 2:30 p.m. the next day. Richardson asked innocuous questions about figure skating, and the talk was interrupted several times because Richardson had to make telephone calls. Once, when Richardson returned from a call, he brought two men and introduced one as Dan Sobolewski of the Detroit office of the FBI. The agent wondered if Harding had a bodyguard service. Gillooly gave him Eckardt's name and information about World Bodyguard Services.

Abruptly, one of the men asked Gillooly who "Derrick" was. "I just about shit my pants," Gillooly said later. But he tried to hide his surprise. Gillooly told the men he didn't know a Derrick. The interview wound down, and Gillooly signed a statement. One of the men said they wanted to speak to Harding on Monday. Before they left, Richardson smiled at Gillooly. You should be proud, he said.

"Behind every great woman is a great man."

That night, Gillooly called Eckardt and warned him to talk to Smith to make sure nothing had gone wrong.

Gillooly fell into a restless sleep. He later told the FBI he woke in the middle of the night and wakened Harding. If the FBI asks about Derrick, he told her, she should say, "You mean Derrick at the ice rink?" and he would say, "That's where I heard that name before." Gillooly had decided he would give up Shawn if it meant protecting himself and Harding. Before sleep returned, Gillooly later told the FBI, Harding said, "We're never going to get out of here, are we?"

Richardson and Sobolewski came to the couple's hotel room the next day. Richardson asked Harding several questions about figure skating but didn't mention the name "Derrick." Harding signed a statement saying she had no knowledge of the attack on Kerrigan. The two investigators gave Harding and Gillooly rides to the airport and said good-bye.

Jim Long had almost forgotten about the telephone message from someone named Crowe.

Long, an investigative reporter for The *Oregonian*, had spent a wonderful, relaxing weekend in Seattle with his wife, Ruby. The two were first-time grandparents and had driven up to visit their new granddaughter for the first time. Long liked to just sit with the tiny Sorayah in his arms. On Saturday evening, holding the sleeping baby, he flipped on the television and happened to catch the final of the women's figure skating championships.

Long knew Harding was from Portland and rooted for her.

"I didn't know anything at all about ice skating, but I knew to cross my fingers when she headed into a difficult jump," Long recalled. "When she landed it, I gave a little cheer— not loud enough to wake the baby. The thing that stuck in my mind was the way Tonya broke her stage-grin at the end of her last big jump and broke into a triumphant smile, knowing she probably had the medal. I was really glad for her."

When Long returned home Sunday, he had a message from the office to call a man named Crowe. Long tried the number, but no one answered, and the reporter wrote it off as one of the many off-beat calls he receives. Long was immersed in other work Monday morning when he remembered the message. He had to call Ruby at home for the number.

This time when Long tried the number, Gary Crowe answered.

Crowe, a longtime Portland private investigator with Billy Ray Cyrus looks and a media-savvy personality, had worked with Long almost twelve years earlier on a software copyright-infringement case. Now, Crowe wanted to give Long first crack at another story.

Crowe taught part-time at Pioneer Pacific College, a small trade school south of Portland. Crowe had been approached by another teacher, a young minister named Eugene Saunders. Saunders was upset and needed to talk.

A student at the school, Shawn Eckardt, had told Saunders about a plot to knock Kerrigan out of the championships. Eckardt played an audio tape—too garbled and poorly recorded to really understand, Saunders said—and identified Gillooly as one of the plotters. The other was a hired hit man from Phoenix.

As Saunders related Eckardt's description of the tape, the conspirators had debated what to do to Kerrigan. The plot was carried out as planned, Eckardt told Saunders. Now Eckardt was afraid that the hit men would come after him for more money, Crowe told Long.

Long asked an editor for a few minutes to check out the story. It would go faster, he said, if he could borrow Dave Hogan, who covered the courts for the newspaper. The two were good friends who often played basketball together on Sunday morning pick-up games—the six-foot-three Long at power forward, the five-foot-eleven Hogan a lightening quick guard. Besides, the two already were working together investigating the loss of $20,000 from an evidence locker at the Portland FBI office. They could quickly check out Crowe's story, then get back to their real work.

Long, Hogan, and Abby Haight, a sportswriter who had covered the recent championships and the assault, gathered in a small meeting room, where Long told Crowe's story. Long and Hogan half-expected Haight to laugh off the tale as too preposterous. She didn't.

"I could see that happening," she said.

Long and Hogan began the basic research into Eckardt and Gillooly. By early afternoon, they had a driver's license, an address, and a telephone number for Eckardt. They wanted to talk to Eckardt but didn't want to scare him off. The reporters decided Haight should call Eckardt to interview him about bodyguard services and, somehow, see if he would reveal anything about the plot. If Eckardt was really that frightened, maybe he'd tell all.

Eckardt didn't sound frightened when he returned Haight's call. He was eager to talk about his work, and they agreed to meet an hour later at a bar in southeast Portland.

The bar, attached to a "family" restaurant near a shopping mall, was almost empty when Haight walked in at 3 p.m. Eckardt, dressed in a dark suit, sat in the back facing the bar's entrance, a cola and a pack of cigarettes on the table in front of him. His choice of tables was planned, he told Haight at the start of their conversation. He saw everyone who came into the bar, and his car—a beat-up 1976 Mercury four-door—waited just outside a nearby emergency door.

For the next two hours Eckardt rambled on about threat assessments, risk evaluations, and observational psychology. As evening neared, a handful of bar patrons ordered drinks, watched a talk show or played video lottery games. Eckardt said he had been recruited by a security company out of college—where he claimed he had studied engineering—and now was the vice president of his own company, World Bodyguard Services. Eckardt talked about his jobs guarding celebrities in Europe, about how he helped Mideast governments battle terrorists and how he was shot at during the strike at the *New York Daily News.*

What did he think of the Kerrigan attack, Haight asked.

"I think it was some nut," Eckardt said. "All I know is there's a lot of weird people out there, and they do a lot of weird things."

He blasted the security at Detroit's Cobo Ice Arena and nearby Joe Louis Arena, where the competition took place. "Where was somebody?" he asked. "In my opinion, security was lacking because it shouldn't have occurred." Midway through the interview, Haight asked Eckardt if he knew the FBI was looking into a plot in Portland to injure Kerrigan so Harding could win the skating championship and get on the U.S. Olympic team. Eckardt brushed past the question.

But as Eckardt's marathon talk wound down, Haight asked him to comment on rumors that he was involved in the plot. "That is absurd," Eckardt said with a surprising lack of anger. "I would never get involved in anything like that. That would jeopardize my future, my career. I mean, that's not something I could do or allow."

Eckardt and Gillooly had driven through Portland to Gillooly's mother's house after Jeff and Tonya's return from Detroit on Monday, January 10. In the car, Gillooly had relayed the gist of his interviews with Detroit authorities. "They asked me who Derrick was, and I just told them I don't know what you're talking about," Gillooly said.

The two cooked up a new coverup, because they knew the questions weren't going away. Eckardt agreed to tell the FBI that he had sent Derrick to Detroit to drum up business for World Bodyguard Services, Inc.; that he hadn't told Jeff about it because he didn't want Jeff to be upset; that it was only after the Kerrigan attack that Gillooly had contacted him to provide security for Harding when she returned from Detroit. Tell the FBI I paid you $3,500 on January 6 for bodyguard services, Gillooly told his friend.

When they arrived at Gillooly's mother's

house, Harding was watching a video of herself skating at the championships. Gillooly went over the alibi with Harding, he later told the FBI. They could explain Harding's calls to the Tony Kent Arena with the same story about getting Kerrigan's autograph on a picture. Gillooly wanted to call Smith and make sure their stories were straight, so the three drove to a nearby gas station to buy a twenty-dollar "talk-and-toss" card. Eckardt slipped into a hotel to make the call, but Gillooly told him to find a less public telephone. They drove to a large department store, where Eckardt called Smith again and went over the story with the Phoenix man. Eckardt told Gillooly he would call Smith on Tuesday and go over the story again.

On Tuesday morning, Harding and Gillooly woke to the jangle of the telephone. Ann Schatz, a reporter for KOIN-TV in Portland, had received an anonymous letter implicating Jeff and Tonya in the assault. Schatz agreed to fax the letter to them; she wanted their comment. The letter arrived about the same time that Eckardt showed up. Gillooly was relieved when he saw the letter because it appeared so "stupid." But the letter had mentioned Derrick's name, and its author had sent a copy to Detroit police.

That afternoon, Gillooly called Sobolewski in Detroit to tell him about the anonymous letter, which he faxed to the agent, along with the letter he had sent to the USFSA complaining about the treatment of Harding's death threat in the fall and the resumes of people providing security for Harding.

Gillooly and Harding then stopped by KOIN-TV for an interview with Schatz. Harding denied any involvement in the assault and said the letter-writer was trying to discredit her. That night, Eckardt went to classes at Pioneer Pacific College. While he stood outside having a cigarette, *Oregonian* reporters Abby Haight and Julie Vader approached him. Did he know the FBI wanted to talk to him, Haight asked. Did he stand by his denial earlier in the day that he wasn't involved?

Eckardt walked away. Of course he knew the FBI wanted to talk to him, he said. And, yes, he stood by his comments.

When Gillooly and Harding arrived at home that night, there were messages from *The Oregonian*. Jeff called Haight, and she told him the paper planned to publish a story that the FBI was investigating Gillooly and others in the plot to hurt Kerrigan. Gillooly thought she meant the anonymous letter, but Haight told him the paper's information came from a different source. Gillooly stayed calm and denied the accusations. As soon as Haight hung up, Gillooly dialed Eckardt's number; Agnes Eckardt said her son couldn't come to the phone; he was talking to two FBI agents.

Harding and Gillooly drove past the Eckardt house several times that night—not knowing they were watched by agents—as Eckardt talked, giving the agreed-upon cover story to the agents. Then one of the agents said they had talked to Saunders, the minister. Eckardt then agreed to tell the truth and the next day became the first of the conspirators to sign a confession.

Later that day, a nervous-sounding Eckardt told Gillooly he wanted to meet him at a local pancake house to talk. Gillooly told the FBI later that he expected that he was being set up, and he told the FBI later that he left his wallet and watch with Harding in the car because he thought he would be arrested. Eckardt wanted to talk money; Gillooly kept his mouth shut, convinced that Eckardt was secretly taping the conversation.

By the end of the day, Derrick Smith also had signed a letter of confession. The following day, both Eckardt and Smith were arrested and charged with conspiracy to commit second-degree assault. On January 14, Stant turned himself in to the FBI office in Phoenix and also signed a confession.

Four days later, an arrest warrant was issued for Gillooly.

10

All Fall Down

After the attack on Nancy Kerrigan in Detroit, reporters were eager to get reactions from other athletes there, including Tonya Harding.

Diane Rawlinson, who was also staying in the Westin Hotel, told The *Oregonian*'s Julie Vader on the phone that she had heard about the attack from Michelle Kwan's coach, Frank Carroll, when they were riding back on a bus from the practice rink. Rawlinson had told Harding about it. Tonya was really upset and frightened, Rawlinson said, and disappointed because "she really wants to skate against Nancy." She went on to say that Harding had had a bad day at practice—a company from Los Angeles had sent the wrong cuts from *Jurassic Park*—the theme music for her long program. "She was not very happy," Rawlinson said.

Tonya couldn't talk, her coach said, because she was taking a nap. But she was supposed to be up by 7 p.m., so call back then.

At 7 p.m. there was no answer in Rawlinson's room, so Vader called the skater directly. Harding answered the phone, sounding grumpy and annoyed. "You weren't supposed to call me. I was sleeping," Harding said.

Vader apologized and said that she had permission from Rawlinson to call. She said she just wanted to know Harding's reaction to the day's extraordinary events.

"I'm really shocked," Harding said. "I don't know what to say. It scares me because it could be anybody there—it could have been anyone and I'm lucky it's not me." She also said that she felt bad for Kerrigan because "we are friends" and then said, again, "It doesn't make me feel very safe."

Asked if she had spoken to Kerrigan since the attack, Harding said no, that she had been sleeping all afternoon.

But what would she say if she could talk to her?

"I'd tell her that I'm really sorry," Harding said. "When it happened to me (the death threat in Clackamas Town Center), it was hard."

In a press conference held the day before the attack, Harding had mentioned that she had hired bodyguards after the death threat in November. But she wouldn't say whether she had a bodyguard with her in Detroit.

In her phone conversation with Vader, Harding said that it didn't seem wise to her to announce whether or not she had protection in Detroit. "Maybe he could have attacked me," she said of Kerrigan's assailant.

The reporter told Harding that it looked as if Kerrigan would recover enough to skate in practice that evening. "I know," Harding said, abruptly "Ann Schatz just told me."

Vader thanked Harding for her time and hung up, momentarily confused. Ann Schatz was a television reporter back in Portland. Why was Harding so grumpy about being awakened by Vader's call if she'd already talked to a reporter on the phone?

The next time Harding talked to reporters was after the ladies' short program on Friday night, January 7. Harding had skated wonderfully, to the theme music from *Much Ado About Nothing*. As is customary, the top finishers were brought into the press conference area, with their coaches.

Not surprisingly, all the reporters wanted to talk about was the Kerrigan assault. The size of the press contingent had swelled with crews from network television and syndicated tabloid shows. Frank Carroll, Kwan's coach, started to tell an interesting story about a man he had seen acting suspiciously at rinkside just before the clubbing—a man whom he described as "sweaty" and, he recalled, who had asked who Nancy Kerrigan was. Carroll said he was annoyed to have someone so close to the skaters who obviously didn't know the sport (later it was determined that the man was simply a reporter).

U.S. Figure Skating Association officials were bothered by the questions and announced that this press conference would be only about skating. As a result, Harding was not asked any direct questions about the attack.

The next day, Harding practiced her long program in Joe Louis Arena. She finished off by landing two very impressive triple axel jumps, and the sparse crowd applauded and whooped in appreciation. Harding obviously was in top form, confident and fit. As Diane Rawlinson made her way from rinkside she noticed Julie Vader sitting in the front row. They smiled and said hello.

"Sorry Tonya was so rude to you," Rawlinson said.

"I'm used to it," Vader replied.

"I'm not," Rawlinson said through a thin smile.

The questions would become harder and harder for Harding when she returned to Portland on January 10. And she would become less and less accessible. She had held a press conference after her triumphant arrival at Portland Airport, but when reporters asked her about the Kerrigan attack, she became visibly annoyed and curt. Why, her attitude seemed to be, were people so intent on spoiling her good time?

The next day, although nothing had yet been published, the walls began to close in on Tonya Harding, Jeff Gillooly, and the others involved.

Television station KOIN had received a copy of a letter from an anonymous woman, who called herself Jane. The letter said that Harding, Gillooly, Eckardt, and others had planned the attack. Reporter Ann Schatz called Harding and asked for an interview about the letter and the growing rumors about the Kerrigan attack. At the skater's request, Schatz faxed the letter to Harding's home.

Harding, Gillooly, and Eckardt read the letter, and then they all went to Eckardt's house. That afternoon, Tuesday, January 11, *Oregonian* photographer Brent Wojahn snapped a picture of the couple leaving the house—a picture that would appear in the morning paper, in the next issue of *People* magazine, and would be broadcast on television. In one hand Tonya Harding holds a cigarette, in the other a pack of Marlboros.

That evening Harding was interviewed for TV cameras about the "Jane" letter.

"I can't believe it," Harding said. "I mean, why does someone want to discredit me? I mean, I just don't understand." She called the letter "totally ludicrous" and said, "I just wish people would see that, you know, I'm out there trying just as much as everybody else is, and it's just really sad. It's sad that there's that kind of people out there."

And she once again expressed her fierce determination. "No one controls my life but me," Harding said. "I mean, if God already wrote it out for me as how it's going to be, but if there's something in there that I don't like, I'm going to change it."

* * *

* * *

After the interview, which was broadcast on the eleven o'clock news, Harding said that she and her husband had stopped at Gillooly's mother's house and then went home. They did not go anywhere else—except out at about three o'clock in the morning to get a copy of *The Oregonian* from someone's driveway. Meanwhile, other stations were broadcasting what was in the early editions of *The Oregonian*.

Harding recounted all this to the FBI in a ten and one-half hour interview in Portland a week later. At least she said that in the first version—the version before the FBI agents told her that lying to a federal agent was a crime and that they knew she was lying.

In her next version of the story to the FBI, Harding admitted that she and Jeff had spent a lot of time driving around that night, trying to call the hit men with Eckardt, trying to get things straightened out. She had not told them this information, she said, because she was afraid of her husband.

That night, when the group, according to their statements to the FBI, were all busy trying to keep the dam from breaking over their heads, Gillooly did take the time to return calls left by reporters for *The Oregonian*.

He told Abby Haight that the whole story of his connection to the plot was absurd. "I have more faith in my wife," he said, "than to bump off her competition."

After the story broke in *The Oregonian*, it seemed as if every reporter in the world wanted to talk to Tonya Harding. Camera crews took up permanent residence in front of every home she might conceivably stay in. There was a blizzard of rumors about where Harding was, where she would be, where she would go. There were rumors that she was going to Virginia for a scheduled appearance in an ice show. Then that she had canceled. Then that she was going. Reporters rushed to the airport in Chicago in the hope that she might be changing flights there.There were rumors that she would talk to "60 Minutes." Or to Diane Sawyer. Or to Barbara Walters. But Harding remained as remote as Garbo.

On Thursday, January 13, Dennis Rawlinson, Harding's lawyer (and husband of Tonya's coach), said that she would have plenty to say. The next day, a statement was issued: "Tonya Harding and Jeff Gillooly are meeting today with their lawyers, Bob Weaver, Dennis Rawlinson, Chris Koback, and Ron Hoevet. Tonya and Jeff have cooperated with law enforcement officials and are in daily contact through their lawyers with the District Attorney's office.

"No arrest warrants have been issued for either of them. In a few days, Tonya and Jeff will have a more detailed statement to present."

It was the beginning of a pattern —brief statements issued through lawyers—vague in both tone and content. And tantalizing off-the-record hints about complete statements to come. Which never did come.

On Sunday afternoon, coach Diane Rawlinson and her husband, Dennis, announced that they would speak to the press in front of their home in the West Hills of Portland. More than one hundred reporters, with five satellite trucks and a dozen television cameras crowded around the house in the quiet neighborhood. Dennis Rawlinson, who had acted as Harding and Gillooly's attorney, came out of the house and distributed a statement. It read: "Tonya Harding categorically denies all accusations and media speculation that she was involved in any way with the Kerrigan assault.

"Tonya is shocked and angry that anyone close to her might be involved. She is pleased to see that Nancy is recovering quickly. She wants the U.S. team to be as strong as possible.

"Tonya is beginning the most important month of the most important year of her life. She wants to represent her country in the Olympics and needs her fans' support and prayers."

After the release was read aloud for the cameras and microphones, Diane Rawlinson declared that Tonya was innocent and that Tonya believed Jeff to be innocent. As for Diane, she was going to stick by her athlete, she believed in her, and together they were going to go to the Olympics.

There are two victims here, Diane declared, Nancy and Tonya. She added that Harding had written a personal letter to Kerrigan, but she did not know its exact contents.

"All I want," Rawlinson told *The Oregonian,* "is for Tonya to be cleared."

That night, in the late hours, reporters gath-

ered at the Clackamas Town Center. Harding
was to skate at midnight, her first practice
since the nationals. She and her husband had
been filmed several times during the past
week, always in cars or on the run. She would
say she was fine or that she was tired and that
she couldn't talk about the Kerrigan case.
Now, in front of a group of specially invited
television crews, she walked into her home
ice rink, her husband by her side, and performed for the cameras. The idea, clearly, was
to get pictures of her skating on television,
not just video of her fleeing from a mob of
reporters.

The next night she practiced again, but this
time Gillooly was absent and Harding looked
upset. Again, she wasn't saying anything—
she wanted her skating to do the talking.

On Tuesday, January 18, Harding put on a
dress and heels and went with her lawyers to
talk to the FBI. The interview would last
more than ten hours, while television crews
and reporters clogged the lobby.

Five times the news pack would catch scent
of its quarry. Five times it bunched forward at
the appointed hour, quarreled over camera
lines and plotted tactics to capture a piece of
Harding. Five times it relaxed as the FBI

announced the interview was being extended. Reporters munched on takeout Chinese food, traded theories and waited. At 9 p.m., Harding finally released a statement to the local media:

"After a lot of agonizing thought and evaluation, I have decided that it would be best for Jeff and me to separate. I am innocent and I continue to believe that Jeff is innocent of any wrongdoing."

Local TV crews went live with the news even as prosecutors put the finishing touches on an arrest warrant that would be served on Gillooly the next day. The slender, unassuming man who had once threatened to break his wife's legs stood accused as the mastermind of the plot to break Kerrigan's.

Finally, at 11:26 p.m., word came that Harding was coming down. More than seventy journalists pressed forward, thrusting cameras and sound mikes that looked like dust mops toward the yellow stripe of tape on the brown tile floor.

The elevator bell chimed. A clump of nervy TV photographers backed out of the jammed elevator cars to a chorus of jeers.

"Down in front, camera down!" shouted photographers whose view of the diminutive athlete was blocked. Harding looked surprisingly fresh, poised—and young. She looked very young.

Harding's clear blue eyes widened as she glanced at what lay in wait. She looked scared, caught in the headlights of a story careening out of control. The kid who dreamed of Olympic gold and the money that comes with it was left with this: Instead of an adoring public, she faced an ugly pack.

Her lawyer, Robert Weaver, told the press that Tonya was exhausted; she would answer questions at the appropriate time. Now was not that time, he said. Weaver grabbed her arm, and Harding tucked her head as the pair wriggled through the crowd.

"Tonya, how are you feeling?" a reporter asked.

"Tired," she said as she ducked by.

The pack became a mob as Weaver and Harding spun through the glass doors and made for the sky bridge and the parking garage. Harding was swallowed by a swarm of cameras and reporters shouting questions. Reporters and photographers, tripping on television cables, sprinted ahead of the beleaguered pair. Shouts erupted when several photographers, backpedaling in front of

Harding, fell in a pile at the first set of stairs. The swarm paused as they scrambled to their feet; the glare of strobes and floodlights painted the night air white.

In the parking garage at last, Weaver barked at the press to stand clear of his car. Someone asked Harding if she had any words for her fans.

"Please believe in me," she said.

The pack swarmed back over the sky bridge like a school of fish to question the authorities. "Was Tonya a suspect?" Meanwhile, Harding, whose latest split with her ex-husband was two hours old, went to her father's apartment in Portland. Early the next morning, reporters watched as Gillooly came out of the apartment and drove away.

The separation from Gillooly did not stop the story. It didn't even slow it down. Tonya was by now a staple of comedy monologues and David Letterman's Top Ten list. She was linked in the opening sketch on "Saturday Night Live" to the maimed John Wayne Bobbitt and the parent-killing rich boys, Lyle and Erik Menendez. She was on the cover of *Time*, *Newsweek*, and *People* and the front page of virtually every newspaper in the country.

Still she wasn't talking to reporters. On Monday, January 24, however, she and her lawyers both issued statements.

"I deny all allegations that I was involved in any way in the Nancy Kerrigan assault.

"As you know, I made myself available to the District Attorney for ten and one-half hours on Tuesday, January 18, 1994. My attorneys continue to work with the District Attorney's office in an effort to resolve this matter as soon as possible.

"As much as I would like to talk to you, I have been directed by my attorneys to remain silent until this matter has been resolved with the District Attorney.

"I have turned my attention to my figure skating and am training regularly in preparation for the Olympics.

"Thank you for your patience and understanding. Your continued support and prayers are appreciated."

For their part, Harding's attorneys said:

"We are pleased that many representatives of the United States Olympic Committee and the United States Figure Skating Association continue to view the allegations against

Tonya with an open mind. We are confident
that the USOC and the USFSA will continue
to abide by their constitution, bylaws, regula-
tions and rules and will deal with this situation in good faith with Tonya's rights and
interests in mind.

"By virtue of her first-place finish at the
U.S. Figure Skating Championships and pur-
suant to the bylaws and rules of the USFSA
and the USOC, Tonya has earned a place on
the U.S. Olympic team. Tonya has done nothing that would warrant her removal from the
team. It would be manifestly unjust and con-
trary to well-established legal principles to
remove Tonya from the team on the basis of
unproven charges.

"Tonya wants us to pass along her best
wishes to Nancy. We all hope Nancy's recov-
ery is quick and complete."

But the press releases did little to divert
interest away from the story or to quell
demands that Harding herself talk about the
matter.

Then, Thursday morning, *Oregonian*
reporters Dave Hogan and Jim Long were
ready to report the basics of what Harding
had said to the FBI during her marathon interview session—that she knew about the plot

and changed her story when talking to federal agents. A few hours before this story was to go to press, Harding's lawyers had called a press conference. At the Multnomah Athletic Club in Portland, Harding read a brief statement her lawyers had prepared for her. She stood on a chair above the bouquet of microphones and read slowly and with emotion.

"I would like to begin by saying how sorry I am about what happened to Nancy Kerrigan. I am embarrassed and ashamed to think that anyone close to me could be involved. I was disappointed not to have the opportunity to compete against Nancy at the nationals.

"I have great respect for Nancy.

"My victory at nationals was unfulfilling without the challenge of skating against Nancy.

"I had no prior knowledge about the assault against Nancy Kerrigan.

"I am responsible, however, for failing to report things I learned about the assault when I returned home from nationals. Many of you will be unable to forgive me for that. It will be difficult to forgive myself.

"When I returned home Monday, January 10, 1994, I was exhausted but still focused on the national championships. Within the next few days, I learned that some persons that were close to me may have been involved in the assault.

"My first reaction was one of disbelief and the disbelief was followed by shock and fear.

"I have since reported this information to the authorities. Although my lawyers tell me that my failure to immediately report this information is not a crime, I know that I have let you down. I have also let myself down. But I still want to represent my country in Lillehammer, Norway, next month.

"Despite my mistakes and my rough edges, I have done nothing to violate the standards of excellence in sportsmanship that are expected in an Olympic athlete.

"Nancy Kerrigan and I can show the world two different types of figure skating. I look forward to being on the team with her.

"I have devoted my entire life to one objective: winning an Olympic gold medal for my country. This is my last chance. I ask only for your understanding and the opportunity to represent my country with the best figure skating performance of my life.

"Thank you."

She stumbled on some words—including the word "sportsmanship"—but it was an impressive performance. Harding did not answer questions, and the entire press "conference" lasted only minutes. Video of the skater reading this statement was broadcast live in Portland and led all national newscasts.

After Harding's statement, what had seemed nearly impossible happened — the story became even bigger. Newspapers across the country devoted whole pages to comments and columns about Tonya Harding's situation.

Everyone, anyone, it seemed, who had ever had any connection with Harding was interviewed. Every television talk show had at least one show devoted to the Harding-Kerrigan case. Harding's old friends, lovers, and roommates debated whether she was the type of person who could do such a dastardly crime. Every television newsmagazine devoted a segment or an entire show to the story. It was almost impossible to turn on television or talk radio and not hear the words "Harding" or "Kerrigan."

Reporters and camera crews from all over the world stayed in Portland for more than a month, providing local hotels and restaurants with an unexpected boost in revenue. The Tonya Harding Fan Club almost doubled in membership. T-shirts, both supporting and deriding Harding, were produced in a hurry.

Kerrigan's handlers were deluged with offers to buy movie rights; "instant books" were written, The *Oregonian's* circulation jumped. Everyone, it seemed, was cashing in on the story of the skater who saw dollar signs when she thought of Olympic gold. But sports agents all seemed to agree: no matter what happened, Harding's value as an endorser was nil.

Clearly, this was more than just a story about a bruise on a knee, more than just a story about competitive zeal. At odds were two cherished, fundamental American principles that, at least on the surface, would seem not to be in conflict at all—the presumption of innocence and the sense of fair play.

With the Winter Games so close at hand, and with a case involving so many venues and so many people, it was clearly impossible for the criminal justice system to work quickly enough to provide Harding with genuine due process before the women's competition began on February 23. Figure skating's governing body, and the Olympic governing bodies, were justifiably afraid of multi-million dollar lawsuits that Harding's lawyers would surely bring if she were prevented from competing before telling her side of the story.

Her lawyers also seemed to want to drag out the investigation, as long as they could keep their client from speaking publicly. Their goals were to get Harding to the Olympic Games and defend her against any possible criminal charges, and both objectives would be helped by Harding's continued silence.

But the evidence against her seemed to grow and grow. When Jeff Gillooly pleaded guilty to racketeering on February 2, and the district attorney's office released the FBI files with Harding's statements and those of her ex-husband and the hit men, all on top of Shawn Eckardt's public confessions, it seemed impossible for the skater to distance herself from the attack on her chief rival.

And yet she did.

Polls showed that while most Americans believed she had something to do with the attack on Nancy Kerrigan, a considerable number of people thought Harding should be allowed to skate in the Olympics anyway, because nothing had been proved. There was a great deal of talk about the apparent abuse Harding had endured as a child and in her marriage. "Tonya is as much a victim as

Nancy" was an oft-heard phrase in Portland and elsewhere.

When Gillooly confessed and said Harding had been part of the plot from the start, he was widely seen as a complete rat. ("Did you hear the headline they wouldn't let me use?" said an *Oregonian* copy editor. "Gillooly the Stoolie.") Some of Harding's fans advanced other scenarios: that Nancy Kerrigan's camp orchestrated the whole thing or that Gillooly had planned and executed it all — the attack, bungled coverup and the confessions — just to get back at Harding. These were dubbed "the grassy knoll theories" in the *Oregonian* newsroom.

Phil Knight, the founder and head of Nike, the shoe company, made a grandstand play of his own. Nike had refused to have Harding as an athlete-endorser years before; now, Knight said, he would contribute $25,000 to pay for Harding's defense of her "right" to compete. Knight, the most powerful shoe salesman in the world, was outraged that sports bureaucrats would even think about suspending an athlete who hadn't been proven guilty in criminal courts. Even President Clinton said he thought Harding should be given the benefit of the doubt.

The climax of the story was all pointing toward Harding on center ice in Lillehammer, dress sparkling in the lights, Olympic rings in the background, waiting for her music to start, ready to skate the performance of her life.

It would be the most-anticipated, most-watched, most-talked about event in sports. It would be the culmination of what Harding has said, repeatedly, is her life's goal. And it would be, without question, one of the most depressing moments the sports world has ever witnessed.

As this book goes to press, the question of whether Tonya Harding will skate in the Olympics is unanswered, but that looks to be the most likely outcome. If she takes the ice in Lillehammer, or marches in opening ceremonies she will be there not because she is the best figure skater in the world, although she is. And she will not be there because she trained hard and performed well and earned a spot on the U.S. Olympic team, although she did.

Tonya Harding will be there because the man she married, and loved, and lived with paid money to thugs so they would whack the current national champion in the leg. Harding will be there because her lawyers threatened to sue to the hilt anyone who tried to prevent her from going.

But most of all she will be there because she doesn't know any better, because she doesn't know what else to do. Tonya Harding learned very early that life is unfair and she has been told, over and over, that life has been particularly unfair to her. She learned that winning is all-important, that it brings love and respect and, especially, money. She learned that violence is a way to solve problems.

For Harding there is nothing else but skating and winning. Of course she wants to win the Olympics, by all means, at any cost. There is no bigger prize. When she wins, then, at last, all things will be put right.

In preparing for that moment, during her public skating sessions at the Clackamas Town Center, Harding drew big crowds of fans, onlookers, and reporters. The shops in the mall's food court did a brisk business.

Harding still refused to talk to reporters about the case, merely offering fleeting comments about skating. She continued to practice her triple jumps and spin control at the same time. And she skated remarkably well.

"She has had two weeks of incredible practices," her coach said. "Right now she is skating better than she has ever skated in her life."

When skaters fall in a heap they must immediately pick themselves up and move their arms to the music and smile and go on as if nothing happened. Everything is fine. If you act as if nothing happened, the judges may forgive or forget the slip.

After the most spectacular fall in her life, Harding was going on as if nothing had happened. She was simply doing what she was trained to do, what she has always done, all her life. She falls down; she gets up.

Her close friend and surrogate father, David Webber, watched her practice for the Olympics and talked about the young woman he knew:

"I've seen both sides of her," Webber said, "and I don't think I have ever seen her as happy as she is now."

Appendix

Statements by Harding and Others

Excerpts of statements given to law enforcement officials by the principals involved in the attack on Nancy Kerrigan. They were released to the public on February 3, 1994, the day Tonya Harding's ex-husband, Jeff Gillooly, pleaded guilty to one count of racketeering in a Portland court. He faced a sentence of 24 months in prison and a $100,000 fine. It was expected Gillooly would serve 19 months for his role in the Kerrigan attack.

TONYA HARDING

On Jan. 18, FBI Special Agent James E. Russell, Detective John Berg of the Multnomah County Sheriff's Office and Norman Frink, chief deputy Multnomah County district attorney, interviewed Tonya Harding in Port-

185

land with her attorney, Robert Weaver.

Tonya Harding began by discussing her on-again, off-again relationship with Jeff Gillooly, whom she divorced in the summer of 1993.

"... Harding stated she and Gillooly got back together during the end of September 1993. She stated they are together now, and she said she considers him her husband. Harding was asked whether Gillooly had ever threatened her, and she stated he had not. ..."

"... Agent Russell asked Harding if she knows Derrick Brian Smith, and Harding said, 'No, I do not.'

"... Agent Russell asked Harding if she knows Shane Stant, and she stated she did not know him....

"... Harding was asked about several telephone calls, which were listed on telephone records....

"At this time, Agent Russell asked Harding ... whether she had been to Eckardt's house at any time on Tuesday night, Jan. 11, 1994. Harding stated she had definitely not been at Eckardt's house during that evening....

"At this time, Agent Russell told Harding that he was sure she had discussed this with her attorney, but Agent Russell asked Harding if she knew the meaning of conspiracy.... Agent Russell asked Harding if she understood, and she said she did.

"Agent Russell then asked Harding if she knew the meaning of hindering prosecution, and she said she did not.... Agent Russell advised Harding that by Oregon law, if she had knowledge that a crime had been committed and did not report that crime to appropriate law enforcement authorities, that was not a violation of Oregon law. However, if she subsequently lied to law enforcement authorities regarding her knowledge of a crime that had been committed, that would be hindering prosecution.... Agent Russell then asked Harding if she was aware that even if she had not committed any crime, that if she lied to an FBI agent, that would be a violation of federal law. Harding stated that she did understand that.

"At this time, Agent Russell told Harding that he knew she had lied to him. He also told Harding that he would tell her exactly how she had lied to him, and at this point, Mr. Weaver stated he wanted to speak privately with Harding....

Frink, Berg and Agent Russell left the interview room so that Harding could confer with her attorneys and later returned.

"... At that time, Mr. Weaver stated Harding had not been totally truthful. He stated he believed Harding honestly had misunderstood some questions, but again said that she had not been totally truthful. Mr. Weaver stated the reason Harding had not been totally truthful was that she is fearful of Jeff Gillooly and his family....

"Mr. Weaver stated Harding was not involved in the planning of the attack. He said that after Harding returned from Detroit, she believed Gillooly was involved in planning the attack on Nancy Kerrigan. Mr. Weaver stated Gillooly never told Harding that he was involved...."

Harding then gave a revised version of the events she had described earlier:

"Harding said that ... on Tuesday, Dec. 28, 1993 ... she dropped Gillooly off at Eckardt's house. Harding said that approximately one hour later, Gillooly called Harding at Gillooly's mother's house to ask Harding to come to get him at Eckardt's house. Harding stated she was driving Gillooly's truck, and Harding recalled that there was a black Porsche ... parked in Eckardt's driveway.

"Mr. Frink asked Harding if her statement

regarding calling the U.S. Figure Skating Association to obtain the telephone number of Kerrigan's skating rink was true, and Harding replied that it was not true. Mr. Frink asked if Harding had made the telephone calls to the rink, and Harding stated that she had not...."

The interview continued with detailed discussion of payments made to Shawn Eckardt and telephone calls made between the subjects of the FBI investigation. The interview ended with this comment from Harding:

"'I just want to say I'm sorry. I hope everyone understands. I'm telling on someone I really care about. I know now he is involved. I'm sorry.'"

VERA MARANO

On Jan. 22, 1994, the FBI interviewed Vera Marano, a free-lance writer who has sold stories to a variety of skating magazines. Marano told agents she had written about Harding and, over time, had become a friend who traded regular phone calls with her.

"Marano did state that ... Harding ... contacted her about two days after Christmas and made the following request. Marano stated that Harding told her that Harding had a 'bet' with someone regarding Nancy Kerrigan and needed the following information: Harding asked Marano if Marano could obtain the name of the facility where Nancy Kerrigan currently trained. She also stated that she wanted to know if Kerrigan owned property in Cape Cod...."

JEFF GILLOOLY

On Jan. 26, 1994, FBI Special Agent James E. Russell and Detective John Berg of the Multnomah County Sheriff's Office interviewed Jeffery Scott Gillooly.

"... Agent Russell asked Gillooly how the idea of doing anything to Nancy Kerrigan first originated and asked whose idea it was. Gillooly stated Shawn Eckardt first came up with the idea....

"... Gillooly explained that during the competition in Japan during December 1993, Harding finished seventh in the technical program and placed fourth at the end of the competition. Gillooly stated Harding was very upset because she thought she skated very well...Gillooly said his discussion with Eckardt prompted Eckardt to say something like 'What if Nancy were to receive some type of threat? Gillooly stated he told Eckardt that it was a good idea. Eckardt stated Tonya should not have knowledge of the plan to do this because she might tell someone. Gillooly said ... that if Tonya was not told, a threat to Nancy would psychologically affect Tonya too. Gillooly stated Eckardt did not like the idea of telling Harding, but Gillooly told Eckardt that Tonya would have to be told.

"... Gillooly stated he asked Harding if it would not be to their benefit if a threat was made against Nancy Kerrigan. Gillooly stated Harding replied that she thought that would be a good idea....

"Gillooly stated Eckardt also told him that Nancy Kerrigan could be taken out of the competition.... Eckardt told Gillooly that Kerrigan's Achilles' tendon could be cut. Eckardt also stated he would do a cost projection.

"... Gillooly told Harding what personal information regarding Nancy Kerrigan that they needed.... Gillooly believes he suggested that Harding call Vera Marano ... to determine Nancy Kerrigan's home address and the skating rink where she trains.

"Gillooly said that on Tuesday, Dec. 28, 1993 ... he drove Harding to Eckardt's house in Gillooly's pickup, arriving at about 11 a.m. Gillooly stated he got out of the pickup, and Harding left in the pickup."

Gillooly told his interviewers that he then went into the house, where he met with Shawn Eckardt, Shane Stant and Derrick Smith:

"... Gillooly told them about Kerrigan's landing leg being her right leg. Eckardt said they would cut her Achilles' tendon, but Gillooly asked if that would not be difficult to do. Derrick said he had a guy in mind, and the guy was a martial arts expert. Derrick said this guy could break Kerrigan's leg with a 'short kick to the long bone' so she would never skate again....

"... Eckardt said something like, 'Wouldn't it be easier just to kill her? Gillooly said, 'No, we're not going to get into that.' Gillooly told them he did not feel comfortable with that, and Derrick agreed with Gillooly. Eckardt stated they could have a guy with a sniper rifle ... and nobody would see that....".

Gillooly said he talked with Harding after the meeting:

"Gillooly stated Harding asked him something like how he felt about it, and Gillooly said he felt pretty good about it but said he would leave it up to Harding. Harding said she would leave it up to Gillooly. Gillooly stated he said something like 'I think we should go for it.' Gillooly stated Harding said something like 'OK, let's do it.'"

Gillooly told agents about delivering money to Shawn Eckardt and about what he said was growing concern because the attack still hadn't taken place. He later met with Eckardt at Clackamas Town Center, a suburban Portland shopping mall, where Harding was practicing:

"Gillooly explained that ... they were standing near the rail of the ice rink, leaning on it, and Harding skated up.... Gillooly stated Harding asked why she could not get someone to do this for her or why it was not getting done, referring to the assault on Nancy Kerrigan. Gillooly stated Eckardt stuttered and then said he did not know why because he did not have enough knowledge of it. Gillooly stated Harding said something like 'If it doesn't get done, you call them and get the $2,000 back.'"

Gillooly then described a later conversation he said he had with Harding:

"Gillooly stated he told Harding that Derrick and Shane were in Detroit and wanted the address of the hotel, address of the skating rinks, Nancy Kerrigan's practice times, and Nancy Kerrigan's room number....

"Gillooly stated he and Harding discussed the situation, and both of them agreed that the room was the best place to attack Nancy Kerrigan....

"Gillooly said that at approximately 12 noon or after on Thursday, Jan. 6, 1994, he was awakened by a telephone call from Harding. Harding said, 'It happened.' Gillooly asked, 'What happened? Harding said, 'Nancy. They did it.' Gillooly said, 'You're kidding.' Harding said, 'No.' Gillooly said, 'Did they get away? Harding said, 'I don't know.'

"Gillooly stated he immediately called Eckardt, and when Eckardt answered, Gillooly said, 'It happened.' Eckardt asked, 'What happened? Gillooly told Eckardt that Nancy Kerrigan was assaulted and that Gillooly did not know if they got away.... Eckardt told Gillooly that Gillooly had better get over to Eckardt's house with some money....

"Eckardt said he had changed world history

or he had altered world history...."

After her Portland interview with the FBI, Tonya Harding called Gillooly:

"Harding told Gillooly that they had been under surveillance since they returned from Detroit. She also told Gillooly that she screwed up the fabricated story in parts and got caught in some of the lies. Harding said she was going to jail. She also told him that the FBI knew that the fabricated story about the reasons for the calls to the Tony Kent Arena in Massachusetts were 'bullshit.'

"... Harding kept assuring Gillooly that she had not implicated him during the FBI interview.

"On Thursday, Jan. 20, 1994, Gillooly said FBI Agent Russell read the notes regarding the interview of Tonya Harding to Gillooly in the office of Gillooly's attorney.... Gillooly said that ... he talked with Harding on the telephone and told her the FBI had read to him the notes that were taken during the interview of her....

"Gillooly told Harding that she implicated him and told her that she should have at least told him that she did. Gillooly said Harding then asked if he meant that the FBI came over and let him look at what they wrote down, in her interview, and Gillooly said yes. Harding then said, 'That's cheating.'"

DERRICK SMITH

On Jan. 12, 1994, the FBI interviewed Derrick Smith at its Phoenix office.

Derrick Smith told agents that Shawn Eckardt called him during the third week of December 1993 and was interested in hiring him to guard Tonya Harding. He said he drove his black Porsche to Portland on Dec. 27. Smith said he took the job and agreed to fly to Detroit, where Harding was competing in the national championships:

"Smith indicated a second reason for going back to the Nationals was to keep an eye on Tonya Harding. Smith was told that he should be very covert as there was a possibility that Harding was running around on Gillooly."

Smith flew to Detroit on Jan. 5 and took a cab to an ice arena where skaters were practicing for the championships. There he met with Shane Stant. The next morning the two went to the arena where the championships would take place. Smith:

"... advised they watched for Harding to

skate and were able to see her practice....
They then drove back to their hotel room....
Smith advised that while watching television
... he recalls seeing television coverage
regarding an attack on Nancy Kerrigan....

"Smith denied that either he or Stant were
involved in the attack...."

The interview ended. Later in the same day
it resumed. Smith said his earlier story was an
alibi he had agreed to with Shawn Eckardt
and Shane Stant. He said he and Stant attend-
ed a meeting at Shawn Eckardt's house Dec.
28:

"Prior to Jeff Gillooly's arrival, Eckardt
indicated that Gillooly wanted someone to
injure Nancy Kerrigan and take her out of the
skating competition....

"Before the actual meeting took place,
Smith asked Eckardt to tape the conversation,
and it was agreed that Gillooly would not
know about this.

"Once the meeting began, Eckardt made
introductions. Smith could tell that Eckardt
was leading Gillooly to believe that Eckardt
was connected to the underground in a major
way, and that he could practically have the
world destroyed if he wanted to....

"Gillooly stated that to do this right, they

needed to injure Kerrigan's right leg, which is her landing leg. Smith suggested hurting her arm, but Gillooly said Kerrigan could skate with an arm in a cast....

"Eckardt promised Gillooly a money-back guarantee, saying that he would give Gillooly his money back if this group was unable to injure Kerrigan....

"Smith saw his role in this whole thing as getting people together. He felt bad about Kerrigan getting hurt, and he told Stant how he felt about it. They agreed that Kerrigan had not done anything to deserve this. They agreed that when this was over, Kerrigan should be OK, or they would not take part in this. They also discussed that they felt Eckardt and Gillooly were going to do this no matter what, and that if they were involved, they could ensure that she was not hurt too badly...."

SHANE STANT

On Jan. 14, 1994, the FBI interviewed Shane Stant at its Phoenix office.

Stant told agents that on Dec. 23 or 24, 1993, Derrick Smith called him and asked if he was interested in a job. Stant said he later received a call from Shawn Eckardt, who told him about the need to "make an accident happen" to a skater.

"Eckardt suggested to Stant that the Achilles' tendon be cut. Stant stated that he declined to do this, as he would not cut anyone...."

Stant said that he and Derrick Smith then drove to Portland, where they met with Shawn Eckardt and Jeff Gillooly at Eckardt's parents' home:

"Jeff Gillooly arrived at the Eckardt residence. Gillooly advised that Tonya Harding had dropped him off.

"Eckardt suggested again cutting her Achilles' tendon. Gillooly suggested that her right knee be injured, because this was the landing leg for skaters...."

Stant told agents he flew to Boston on Dec. 28, hoping to club Nancy Kerrigan while she practiced at her home arena. He never found her, however, and took a bus to Detroit. He met Derrick Smith on Jan. 5, and the two planned to attack Kerrigan at the skating arena where the national championships would take place. Stant carried a note, written to make it appear that a psychotic was stalking skaters, and an ASP, a retractable police baton. He watched Kerrigan practice and moved in to make the hit:

"He walked to the right of Nancy Kerrigan, who was talking with another female. He took the ASP out in his right hand and put the note in his left hand. Stant then proceeded toward Kerrigan and struck her a glancing blow with the ASP on her right leg, approximately one inch above the joint. Stant stated that she immediately hit the ground. Stant stated that he hit her with approximately half his force.... He continued to move and dropped the note. He then began to pick up his pace to a run toward the glass doors he had seen before. He arrived near a table and noticed that the doors were chained together. He then ran through the bottom of the door like a football tackle. This popped the Plexiglass out of the door. At this point Stant stated that he heard someone say, 'Somebody stop him.' ... He started running down the street, and a man got in his way, whom he knocked down.... During the run he threw the ASP under a car, into the snow.... Smith pulled up alongside him, and he entered the car and they drove off...."

An FBI agent asked Stant if the conspirators had made arrangements for an alibi:

"Stant stated that Smith had discussed this with him.... Their response to any questioning would be that they had been hired by Gillooly to discover if his wife had been cheating on him...."

Exclusive Interview with Harding's Bodyguard

Shawn Eric Eckardt, Tonya Harding's sometime bodyguard, sat for a three-hour interview with Oregonian *columnist Phil Stanford. It was the first interview Eckardt gave after his arrest on January 13, 1994. The interview appeared over two days, January 20 and 21, and is reproduced below.*

Shawn Eric Eckardt, the very hefty 26-year-old bodyguard, says the plot against skating star Nancy Kerrigan began last month with a visit to his office by Jeff Gillooly.

As Eckardt explained it in a three-hour interview with The Oregonian, Gillooly - then the manager and on-again, off-again husband of Kerrigan's rival, Tonya Harding - was an old friend of his. They'd known each other for

21 years. Over the past five or six years, Eckardt says, he had provided sporadic security advice to Harding and Gillooly on an informal basis. Gillooly never paid him for his services, he says, but on occasion he and Harding would take Eckardt out for dinner.

The best Eckardt can remember, the December visit from Gillooly was probably on the 16th or 17th. At the time, Eckardt explains, he was operating his fledgling security business, World Bodyguard Services Inc., from a room on the second floor of his parents' house in a section of Portland called Lents:

It was in the daytime. I don't remember exactly what time it was. And he, you know, asked me if there was any way that I could find somebody to, you know, disable Nancy Kerrigan.

Is that the word he used - disable?

Well, make it so she couldn't skate. That was more like the phrase he used. He asked me if I knew anybody, and I said, "Well, I know a

couple of guys who might, you know, do
something like that. Let me check around. . . ."

Did you know who Nancy Kerrigan was at the
time?

Well, he said that Nancy Kerrigan was the
girl that Tonya had to beat to win nationals
and go to the Olympics.

And then he said, you know, when this hap-
pens, the skating world will be in an uproar
and, you know, because sports are becoming
more violent ... he would have to end up hir-
ing the corporation that I had at the time,
World Bodyguard Services Inc., to provide
protective services.

And then he said I'd make a lot of money.
Things like, "How's it gonna feel driving that
brand new ZR1 Corvette-" And, "What's it
gonna be like having an office suite in one of
the downtown buildings-" and all that other
stuff.

I said if I find anybody, I'll let you know. But
time went by, and I didn't actively pursue
looking for anyone. And then one day, I got a
call from a friend of mine, Derrick Smith, who
had recently moved to Phoenix.

As Eckardt recalls, the call from Smith came around the 20th or 22nd of December - in any case, during the week before Christmas. Smith, who is 29, was another longtime friend of Eckardt's. The two of them shared a common interest in international espionage and paramilitary activities of all sorts. In fact, the two of them had previously discussed Smith's plans to start an anti-terrorist academy somewhere around Phoenix.

As it developed, Smith was calling to see whether Eckardt could come to Phoenix to help get the anti-terrorist academy off the ground. However, at some point, Eckardt recalls, Smith asked him whether anything else was going on. At that point, Eckardt says, he told Smith that Gillooly had asked him to find someone to disable Nancy Kerrigan. Would he be interested?

And Smith says, "Sure, we can do it. ... How much is the job worth?"

Eckardt tells him $6,500 because that, he says, is the figure that he and Gillooly had decided on.

"Yeah, we can do it for that," Smith says, "We'll pay Shane $4,000, and he'll do it."

This is the first time Shane Minoaka Stant's name crops up. Stant, who is Smith's nephew and another paramilitary type, also lives in Phoenix.

On Dec. 27 or 28, Smith and Stant show up in front of Eckardt's parents' home in Stant's black Porsche 944. Time is a-wasting, Smith says, and they want an audience with Gillooly the next day. The meeting is set for 10 a.m. in the second-floor corporate offices of World Bodyguard Services Inc.

Well, Jeff didn't show up until 11. And then, while we were waiting, Derrick Smith asked me to tape the conversation so that he would be able to have leverage against Jeff at a later date. I put the tape recorder on the desk and put a paper towel over it.

And then Jeff came over, and we made the introductions and I sat down. Derrick told Jeff that he had come up from Phoenix to talk to him about this problem, and how he was the kind of guy who takes care of people's problems. And then Jeff told them what he wanted done. Stant ... he was standing in the corner ... wearing his baggy Australian out-back coat, you know, with this gun sticking in his belt.

When Smith told Gillooly he was here to help him, what did Gillooly say he wanted done?

He told him how we was looking for someone to make sure that Nancy Kerrigan didn't skate in the nationals.

How specific did he get?

Well, he didn't. We started bouncing around ideas from one spectrum to the other. We started using terms like, well, "Why don't we get rid of her-" "We'll get rid of her" and stuff like that.

And then I really didn't want to be involved in any murder conspiracy or anything. I mean, that just sort of red-flagged it in my mind right then. And we sorta basically sorta moved away from that.

How? What else did anyone say?

Well, I said, "We don't need to do that ..." And Jeff said, "What can we do less than that-" And we started bouncing ideas around, like, well, you know, the standard ... I mean the sort of things that you would see in the movies. Like, you know, damage to the hamstrings and Achilles' tendons and things like that.

One idea that was mentioned was: Let's get her in a car accident and bruise her up a bit. She can't skate with cracked ribs and stuff like that.

And then Jeff mentioned, well, her landing leg. If you do anything to her landing leg, she can't do a jump. She can't skate.

And then Jeff said: "Yeah, that's it. Why don't we just break her landing leg. Just break her right leg.

"It's a perfect idea! Disable her landing leg! She won't be able to skate!" he said ...

"Yeah," says Smith, "we'll break her leg."
So Jeff and Derrick sort of shook hands and agreed that Derrick would do the service and that Jeff would pay him $6,500 to do it. And then Derrick Smith and Shane Stant left.

Jeff had to wait because Tonya had to come pick him up, because she had dropped him off. And when he left he was all excited and bubbly about all this money he was going to make.

Later that day, Eckardt says, Gillooly returned to drop off $2,000 in cash, which he handed to Smith. Smith spent the rest of the day playing with Eckardt's computer, trying to get information about Kerrigan. That evening he drove Stant to Seattle to catch a plane to Boston.

According to Eckardt, everyone was excited about the vistas that appeared to be opening up in front of them - and not just because of the obvious effects their plot would have on Tonya Harding's skating career.

The way they saw it, if they just took the plan a step farther, they would all soon be rolling in money.

As Eckardt recalls, in the course of the Dec. 28 meeting where the attack was plotted, Smith and Gillooly also came up with the idea of leaving a note behind, suggesting that the attack was the act of a crazed individual who was stalking all the top international skating stars.

So they said, "Well, why don't we just throw a note on her or drop a note saying there's going to be more threats?"

Smith liked the idea because it would possibly open up the doors for more business. You know, he wanted to take the proceeds from the protective service operations and open up this training facility in Arizona that he wanted to put together so bad, and he wanted me to run it for him.

So, anyway, we came up with this note that was supposed to be dropped - thrown at Kerrigan or whatever. It was supposed to name the other targets.

Who were the other targets?

Well, Tonya's name was on it. Kerrigan's name was on it and some other people I don't recall. Derrick told me: Just cut (letters) out of magazines and paste them together. But I would like to reiterate that there were never additional attacks thought of, or construed, or even considered.

Basically, it just implied that a psychotic

stalker individual was out there stalking these figure skaters.

It was, you know, the sole intent of the letter to provide a psychological effect within the skating community. And Derrick Smith liked the idea because it would open up doors for him.

Meaning that there would be a demand for protective services?

Yeah. And that's what he wanted to do, you know. And Jeff keeps going: "Yeah, you guys will be the bodyguards to the figure skaters." And he also thought that by leaving a note of that type it would detract from any attention that might be put on any possible suspects. You know, like Tonya.

Do you know if the note was ever delivered?

No.

As Eckardt recalls, as soon as Stant reached Boston, problems began surfacing. Smith, back in Phoenix, was calling every day or so, demanding more money, which he said Gillooly had promised. However, when Eckardt relayed the messages to Gillooly, Gillooly told him he wasn't paying any more money until he saw some results. What was Stant doing, anyway?

Smith, who had told Eckardt that he, and he alone, was Stant's "control agent," passed back the message that the reason Stant wasn't doing anything was that he didn't have enough money to rent a car.

Gillooly began to press Eckardt, asking if Stant really was in Boston or whether the two of them - Smith and Stant - were sitting back in Phoenix with his $2,000. Eckardt says he was beginning to have some doubts of his own.

Gillooly, who steadfastly refused to talk directly to Smith, demanded through Eckardt that Smith produce some receipts to prove that Stant was in Boston. Smith, for his part, threatened to do bodily harm to Gillooly.

Eckardt, as he describes it now, was already getting tired of the cloak-and-dagger business. But now he was caught in the middle and didn't know how to get out.

Finally, says Eckardt, Gillooly told Eckardt

to come to the Clackamas Town Center skating rink in suburban Portland, to meet with him while Harding was holding one of her midnight skating practices. Eckardt says that during this time, Gillooly requested his presence at the sessions twice. One of the times, he believes, was Dec. 31.

On that night, Eckardt, who was suffering from severe back problems that put him in the hospital from time to time, "popped a couple of Vicodin" - a presciption painkiller - and drove to the rink.

Gillooly took him aside.

He says, "I need you to go out and find somebody who can actually do it." And he says: "Offer them a lot of money. Tell these guys I'll give them a $10,000 bonus if they'll get it done."

And then he pulls out this $10,000 check from the United States Figure Skating Association. And I'm debating whether or not I should even bother with it. I should just let these guys break his legs. ...

"I want receipts," Gillooly says. "I want them to prove to me that there's somebody back there."

And I say, "OK, I'll let Derrick know."

At one of these midnight sessions, Eckardt says, Gillooly informs him that he has Harding's permission to spend the money on the operation. He says he was sitting on some steps next to the rink at the time, and Harding came skating up.

She said, "Hi, how's your back- How're you feeling-" I said, "Oh, not really well." I feel like I'm drunk because I'm on my pain medication.

And then she said that she was pissed off and disappointed that these guys weren't able to do what they said they were gonna do. And why hasn't it happened yet.

But as the whole world knows by now, there was no attack in Boston. Smith called Eckardt, informing him that he had sent Stant to Detroit, by Greyhound bus, where the nationals were being held. At first, Eckardt says, Gillooly was annoyed, but soon he got used to the idea. After Stant left a message on Gillooly's recorder - "Jeff, this is Shane - I'm in Detroit" - he says Gillooly was actually happy, because he finally had proof that someone was on the job.

At this point, Eckardt says, the plan was to "do" Kerrigan in her hotel room. According to Eckardt, Gillooly wanted Stant to attack Kerrigan there. He says Harding identified the hotel for them.

"Jeff wanted this guy to go to her room and do his business with her and then leave. And duct-tape her up so she wouldn't be able to call out - so they'd find her in the morning with a damaged leg of some sort, wrapped up in duct tape."

Eckardt and Gillooly wired $750 to Smith in Phoenix so he could be in Detroit for the end of the competition. Later they sent $1,300 to Detroit.

On the morning of Jan. 6, at about 10 a.m., Eckardt says he was awakened by a call from Gillooly who told him that he'd just heard that Nancy Kerrigan had been attacked. Somebody had come up to her and broken her leg.

About an hour later the phone rang again, and it was Smith. "Hey," Eckardt remembers

Smith saying, "you should have seen what I saw on the news. When Kerrigan was coming out of her practice session, somebody came up and hit her on the leg and took off."

About an hour or so later, as Eckardt remembers it, he was watching the television himself, and there was Nancy Kerrigan lying on the floor, screaming and crying. He says he went into the bathroom and threw up.

"I was very upset," he said. "I couldn't believe I had done this ... I just kept seeing the same scene over and over again. Kerrigan was sitting on the ground, screaming and crying, 'Why me? Why me?' "

There was, however, no time for Eckardt to indulge his sorrow. The day after the attack, Smith called him from Detroit, asking for money.

As Smith put it to Eckardt, if he didn't get $1,250 fast, Stant would have to become a permanent resident of the Motor City.

So once again Eckardt called Gillooly, who came over to his house with $1,300. Together the two of them drove to the Cub Foods store on Southeast 82nd Avenue in Clackamas, south of Portland, and wired the money to

Smith.

The next day Smith was on the phone again, demanding more money. This time the sum in question was $4,600, which, says Eckardt, is the amount that Smith figured Gillooly still owed him. Once again Eckardt relayed the request to Gillooly. Gillooly said they'd have to get back to him.

Before that could happen, though, Gillooly was on a plane to Detroit, where that Saturday night Harding would win the national figure skating championship. Eckardt said that Gillooly wanted to take him along, too, to provide security for Tonya, but didn't have enough money for another ticket.

Monday night, January 10, when Harding and Gillooly returned to Portland, Eckardt was at the airport to greet them. He ushered her into her father's truck, which was waiting outside. "Go, go, go!" he yelled. He and Gillooly left the airport in his car.

"We gotta talk," Gillooly said. Then he told Eckardt that the FBI had questioned him.

"They asked me who Derrick was," Gillooly said. "And I just told them I don't know what you're talking about."

Gillooly said the FBI had also asked about Eckardt. They had asked for a description and were apparently disappointed when Gillooly told them Eckardt weighed about 330 pounds. They were looking for someone more in the neighborhood of 220 - about what Shane Stant weighs.

At this point the authorities hadn't got the cast of characters straight yet. But they were closing in. They knew someone named Derrick was involved.

"Where did they get the name?" Gillooly wanted to know.

Eckardt knew, but he wasn't about to tell Gillooly.

A couple of days before the attack on Kerrigan, Eckardt had played his tape recording of the conspirators meeting on Dec. 27 or 28 for a fellow student by the name of Eugene Saunders. As Eckardt tells it now, he did so in hopes that Saunders, a minister, would go to the authorities. Saunders had obviously told somebody.

"No," Eckardt told Gillooly, "I don't know where they got the name. I didn't tell anybody."

At Harding's father's house, Gillooly and

219

Harding got in their truck and drove home. Eckardt followed after them with the luggage. Inside their house in Beavercreek, a rural area southeast of Portland, Eckardt says, Gillooly brought the subject up again. At first, he says, Harding just sat there, listening:

Jeff kept saying how we were all going to go to jail. And, you know, I'm sitting there listening, and Tonya was getting upset. And then she started coming up with these excuses for the acts that she had done.

She had made several phone calls back to the (arena) in Boston to try and find out how to get ahold of Kerrigan. And she said she was going to use the excuse that she had this poster with herself, Kristi Yamaguchi and Nancy Kerrigan on it. She had signed the poster, and Yamaguchi had signed the poster, but she needed Kerrigan's signature on it because she was going to send it to a fan.

The wheels were spinning in Gillooly's head too, Eckardt recalls. "What are we going to do?" he kept asking. Finally he hit upon it: They would say that Derrick — the one name they knew the FBI had — had gone to Detroit to drum up business for Eckardt's protective service company.

He wanted me to tell the FBI that I had surreptitiously sent Smith back on a sort of marketing expedition — to market to Claire Ferguson of the (U.S. Figure Skating Association) and some of the other figure skaters. And he told me to make sure I told the FBI that I did not tell Jeff because I didn't want to (anger him) and lose the potential contract with him . . . .

"OK," he said, "let's get a hold of Smith and get our stories straight."

And so, Eckardt said, they went off to call Smith. Of course, they wanted to make the call from a pay phone. But to do so they had to get a disposable credit card. At 1:30 in the morning this was not the easiest thing to do. Finally they found one at Jubitz Truck Stop on Marine Drive in Portland.

Wednesday morning, Eckardt was awakened by his mother banging on his bedroom door. She said that Harding had called and it was an emergency. "You gotta get out there now."

So Eckart showered, threw on his clothes and raced out to their home. Gillooly and Harding had a copy of *The Oregonian* with a story breaking the first news of the scandal.

"We've got to get some damage control," Gillooly said. "I'm great at damage control." According to Eckardt, Harding was completely calm. "She's not worried," Eckardt said. "She told me . . . that she had absolutely convinced herself that she had done nothing wrong — and if she maintains the same state of denial that Jeff did, that everything would be OK."

Eckardt, himself, was not so positive about that. That night when two FBI agents showed up at his house, at first he gave them the agreed-upon cover story. They listened politely.

Then one of them said, "Shawn, do you know it's against the law to lie to an FBI agent?"

"Well, yeah."

"Do you know what a conspiracy is?"

Eckardt nodded.

And then one of them — John King, as Eckardt recalls — said, "Do you know Eugene Saunders?"

And that, Eckardt said, is when he knew the

game was up. "Come on," said King, "We know all about it. Why don't you tell us what really happened."

And that, said Eckardt, is exactly what he did.

Acknowledgements

While J.E. Vader and Abby Haight wrote this book, many people helped produce the research, reporting and photography that went into it. During January and early February 1994, *The Oregonian* threw an enormous portion of its resources at the Nancy Kerrigan/Tonya Harding story. The result was exclusive, timely and comprehensive coverage. Inevitably, someone deserving will be inadvertently left off the list that follows. But this was truly a team effort of everyone at the newspaper: in the newsroom, in its production departments, in its circulation operation and its administrative departments. Among the contributors to the coverage:

Reporters and writers: Dave Hogan, James Long, Phil Manzano, Tom Hallman Jr., Brian T. Meehan, Bill MacKenzie, Ken Wheeler, John Painter Jr., Ashbel S. Green, Fred Leeson, Dan Hortsch, John Snell, Peter Sleeth,

Kathie Durbin, Barnes C. Ellis, Aaron Fentress, Risa Krive, Jim Hill, Bethanye McNichol, Steve Woodward, Roberta T. Ulrich, Stuart Tomlinson, Erin Hoover, Dwight Jaynes, Phil Stanford, Margie Boule, Norm Maves Jr., Pete Schulberg, Terry Richard, James Mayer, Web Ruble, Rose Ellen O'Connor, Richard Cockle, Jennifer Brandlon, Paul Pintarich and Marty Hughley.

Editors: Executive Editor Sandra M. Rowe, Managing Editor Peter Bhatia, Therese Bottomly, Dennis Peck, John Killen, Galen Barnett, Jim Camin, John Harvey, Michael Rollins, David Austin, Kathy Nokes, Jill Thompson, Mary Joan O'Connell, Doug Bates, John Hamlin, Larry Kurtz, Tad Davis, and other editors of *The Oregonian*'s city desk, news copy desk, sports desk and features desk.

Photographers: Doug Beghtel, Marv Bondarowicz, Benjamin Brink, Patricia Cordell, Joel Davis, Bob Ellis, Roger Jensen, Michael Lloyd, Steve Nehl, Angela Cara Pancrazio, Elaine Schumake, Dale Swanson, Tom Treick and Brent Wojahn.

Photo editors: Serge McCabe, Randy Rasmussen, Kraig Scattarella, Ross Hamilton and Claudia J. Howell

Artists: Michelle Wise, Ngoc Wasson, Kevin Hendrickson, Rene Eisenbart

Researchers: Gail Hulden, Sandy Macomber, Kathy Blythe and Carol McMenamin

ABBY HAIGHT, a Northwest native, was a news reporter for six years before joining *The Oregonian* as a sportswriter in 1990. She has been reporting figure skating and Tonya Harding for two years.

J.E. VADER became a sports columnist for *The Oregonian* in January 1993. She has covered figure skating for eight years, first as a reporter for *Sports Illustrated* and then as a staff writer for *The National* sports daily.

The Oregonian, in a January 12, 1994, story by reporters James Long and Dave Hogan, broke the story of the involvement of those close to Tonya Harding in the plot against Nancy Kerrigan. It subsequently was the first to report virtually every development in the case.

The Oregonian, based in Portland, has been published since 1850 and is available throughout the state of Oregon and much of the Pacific Northwest, an area of more than 100,000 square miles. The paper circulates 350,000 copies daily and 460,000 on Sunday.